Figuratively Speaking

Covers 40 Basic Literary Terms Using Examples from Classic Literature

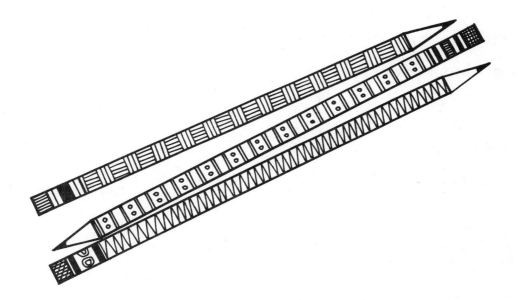

by Delana Heidrich

illustrated by Bev Armstrong

2004 · The Learning Works

The Learning Works

Editor: Kimberley A. Clark
Illustrator: Bev Armstrong
Book design: Eric Larson, Studio E Books
Art director: Tom Cochrane
Cover design: Barbara Peterson
Cover illustration: Rick Grayson
Project director: Linda Schwartz

Contents

Introduction

Relying on your school district's core literature textbooks can make teaching literary terms and techniques a hit-or-miss experience. Three stories in a row may demonstrate the characteristics of *symbolism* while a clear example of an *oxymoron* may be missing from the entire text.

Your fifth- through eighth-grade students cannot afford to receive hit-or-miss coverage of literary terms and techniques. End-of-the-year standardized tests will evaluate their understanding of basic terms. Future high school and college courses will demand they interpret and employ literary terms and techniques. Post-school experiences will require them to evaluate values and beliefs that they can first encounter in classic literature.

Organized into "Figurative Language," "Poetic Language," and "Literary Techniques," the book draws on classic literature to illustrate and instruct in the use and understanding of basic literary terms. Three pages are dedicated to each of forty literary terms. The first page of each lesson includes a definition of the term and one or more samples from grade-appropriate classic literature. The next two pages challenge students to identify and understand the term and use it on their own.

Use *Figuratively Speaking* to introduce or review literary terms and techniques. Tie the lessons together into an entire unit or pull out individual activities as they apply to lessons you present throughout the school year. However you use *Figuratively Speaking*, your students will be challenged with exciting and interactive activities that thoroughly instruct on the understanding and use of literary terms and techniques.

Denotation and Connotation

Definitions

Denotation: The dictionary definition of a word. "America" denotes the country south of Canada and north of Mexico.

Connotation: The thoughts, feelings, and images associated with a word. "America" connotes freedom, individualism, and opportunity.

Examples from Literature

Henry Wadsworth Longfellow recognizes both the dictionary definitions and the connotations of *spring* and *autumn* in the first stanza of "Autumn Within":

> It is autumn; not without
> But within me is the cold.
> Youth and spring are all about;
> It is I that have grown old.

In his autobiography, author Pio Baroja uses the word *rain* to connote troubles and hardships. In this passage, he refers to the first of many frustrations in his life:

> When I first went to school in Sebastian, at the age of four—and it has rained a great deal since that day—the teacher...looked me over and said: "This boy...will never amount to anything."
> —Pio Baroja, *Youth and Egolatry*

A generation earlier, *rain* connoted the same feelings of sorrow and disappointment:

> Into each life some rain must fall,
> Some days must be dark and dreary.
> —Henry Wadsworth Longfellow, "The Rainy Day"

Understanding Denotation and Connotation

On another sheet of paper, answer the following questions in one or two paragraphs.

1. What do the words *spring* and *autumn* denote? What do they connote? Study the first stanza of "Autumn Within" to help you decide. What does the word *cold* connote in the same poem?

2. In "The Rainy Day," Longfellow suggests that "some days must be dark and dreary." What does the word *dark* denote? What does it connote?

3. In 1858, Hans Christian Andersen wrote a fairy tale called "Something." The eldest of four brothers begins the story by saying, "I mean to be somebody and do something useful in the world." What does it mean to "be somebody"? What does it suggest when someone says, "I'm just a nobody"?

4. Edgar A. Guest defines "home" in his poem of the same name:

   It takes a heap o' livin' in a house t' make it home.

   What images, feelings, and thoughts do you associate with the word *home*?

Identifying Denotations and Connotations

Match each of the following words with its denotation and its connotation. Place the appropriate letters in the spaces provided to show your answers.

	Denotation	Connotation	Denotations	Connotations
1. cherub	_____	_____	a. the son of a king	f. ambitions and desires
2. prince	_____	_____	b. light from the sun	g. innocent and childlike
3. fox	_____	_____	c. a wolf-like mammal	h. noble and admirable
4. dream	_____	_____	d. an angel	i. clever or sneaky
5. sunshine	_____	_____	e. visions during sleep	j. warmth and happiness

Recognizing Negative and Positive Connotations

Imagine you are a business person trying to come up with store names and slogans that convince shoppers to buy your products. Words and phrases that carry positive connotations can help you improve your sales. Below are listed pairs of store names and advertising slogans. Decide which name or slogan in each pair carries positive connotations. Circle the positive slogans and phrases.

Store Names	**Advertising Slogans**
1. The Bargain Barn	5. We sell high-priced shoes.
A Shack of Cheap Stuff	We carry only the highest quality footwear.
2. Used Cars, Inc.	6. Cheap clothes for sale.
Vintage Automobiles	Clothes at a price you can afford.
3. Worms and Hooks	7. Coziest cabin on the market today.
The Ol' Fishin' Hole	Tiny house for sale.
4. Pasta Paradise	8. Our workers are all computer nerds.
Sloppy Noodles	We employ highly skilled technicians.

Writing Tip

When writing anything from poetry to persuasive essays, from narratives to informational prose, select words that carry not only the correct dictionary definitions, but also the connotations that will help your audience feel or imagine the meaning you intend.

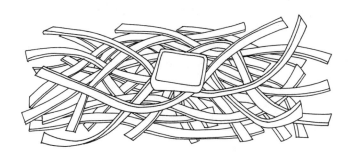

2 Hyperbole

Definition

Hyperbole: Obvious exaggeration used to emphasize a point or add excitement and humor to a story.

Examples from Literature

Tall tales make real and fictional heroes seem larger-than-life by using hyperbole. Since many hero stories are passed down orally, the tales get taller with each telling.

Hyperbole that begins with a real-life character stretches a fact until it becomes fiction. Johnny Appleseed, for example, actually did walk barefoot often. His feet really did become callused and tough. Yet, his friend's suggestion that it would kill a rattlesnake to bite into the toe of Johnny Appleseed was pure hyperbole.

Hyperbole dealing with fictional characters can go even further. Pecos Bill is said to have ridden a tornado like any other cowboy would ride a horse. His wife is said to have ridden a catfish as large as a whale.

Mark Twain makes use of hyperbole to describe an eager betting man in "The Celebrated Jumping Frog of Calaveras County":

> If he even see a straddlebug start to go anywheres, he would bet you how long it would take him to get to—to wherever he was going to, and if you took him up, he would foller that straddlebug to Mexico but what he would find out where he was bound for and how long he was on the road.

Identifying Hyperbole

Davy Crockett was a frontiersman and storyteller. In 1834, he wrote a semifictional autobiography. Underline the phrases in these passages from his story that illustrate hyperbole.

> The next morning…we had just eat our breakfast, when a company of hunters came to our camp, who had fourteen dogs, but all so poor that when they would bark they would almost have to lean up against a tree and take a rest.
> I took a notion to hunt a little more, and in about one month I killed forty-seven more, which made one hundred and five bears I had killed in less than one year.
> We had laid down by our fire, and about ten o'clock there came a most terrible earthquake, which shook the earth so, that we were rocked about like we had been in a cradle…we thought it might take a notion and swallow us up, like the big fish did Jonah.
>
> —Davy Crockett, *A Narrative of the Life of David Crockett of the State of Tennessee*

Understanding Hyperbole

Paul Bunyan is said to have been such a large infant that he slept in a covered wagon instead of a crib. As an adult, he supposedly used tree trunks as toothpicks and wagon wheels as buttons. In today's world, how might Paul Bunyan get along? List things that could be used by such a giant for each of the items below.

1. toothbrush   _____
2. hat   _____
3. shoes   _____
4. dinner   _____
5. umbrella   _____
6. baseball and bat   _____
7. lunchbox   _____
8. bed   _____
9. pencil and paper   _____
10. table   _____

Explaining Hyperbole

On another sheet of paper, answer the following questions in one or two paragraphs.

1. Why does the use of hyperbole add excitement to a story? Why does it add humor?

2. When is hyperbole appropriate? Should a politician use hyperbole when telling voters what he or she will do if elected? Why or why not? Should an advertiser use hyperbole in describing a product? Why or why not?

3. Describe a visual hyperbole you have seen in a cartoon, movie, or television program.

Using Hyperbole

Use exaggeration to write your own tall tale by filling in the blanks below.

In the great village of _____ lived a superhuman hero named

_____. Our superhero had this incredible ability to

_____ .

One day _____

_____ .

The whole town was worried until_____

_____ .

In the end, everything turned out well because _____

_____ .

It pays to have a superhero live in your village!

Reading and Writing Exercise

Find a work of satire, such as a Dave Barry column, in the newspaper. Notice how satires use hyperbole to add humor and absurdity. Choose a sport, holiday, song, movie, or event to make fun of and write about this topic using hyperbole to create your own work of satire.

3 Idiom

Definition

Idiom: An expression that means something different from what it says. Idioms are culturally based. The British and the Americans, for example, speak the same language but may not understand each other's idioms.

Examples from Literature

Norton Juster's classic work *The Phantom Tollbooth* is filled with colorful word plays. In this passage, the king of a land called Dictionopolis uses idioms in boasting of the talents of his cabinet members to Milo, the book's main character:

> "Why, my cabinet members can do all sorts of things. The duke here can make mountains out of molehills. The minister splits hairs. The count makes hay while the sun shines. The earl leaves no stone unturned. And the undersecretary," he finished ominously, "hangs by a thread. Can you do anything at all?"

Mark Twain added color to his stories with the use of idioms, too. In his tale *A Story Without an End,* the following idioms were showcased:

> Sailors…*wrestled with the tale.*
>
> …nobody *was stirring.*
>
> Mary Taylor…was *all in all* to him.
>
> He *took to the road.*
>
> …his *hopes were high.*
>
> They *were all moved.*
>
> He would…*win the mother over.*
>
> Mrs. Enderby *had the best head* for planning.

Defining Idioms

On another sheet of paper, define the following idioms from Mark Twain's *A Story Without an End*:

1. Sailors…*wrestled with the tale.*
2. Mary Taylor…was *all in all* to him.
3. …his *hopes were high.*
4. He would…*win the mother over.*
5. …nobody *was stirring.*
6. He *took to the road.*
7. They *were all moved.*
8. Mrs. Enderby *had the best head* for planning.

Illustrating Idioms

On a separate piece of paper, illustrate the literal meaning of one of the idioms from *The Phantom Tollbooth* (or another idiom listed here). Below your picture, write the intended meaning of the idiom. Finally, challenge your classmates to guess which idiom you have illustrated.

Idiom List

The duke makes mountains out of molehills.
The count makes hay while the sun shines.
The undersecretary hangs by a thread.
He bends over backwards to get his work done.
It's right on the tip of my tongue.
I have a splitting headache.

The minister splits hairs.
The earl leaves no stone unturned.
I'm sitting on top of the world.
You drive me up the wall.
That will cost an arm and a leg.
Here's food for thought.

Milo's Response

In *The Phantom Tollbooth*, Milo is asked: "Can you do anything at all?" Reread the talents of the cabinet members in Dictionopolis. Then write an idiom that might define one of the talents of a young boy.

Your idiom: _____

_____

_____ .

Using Idioms

Since idioms add humor, they are not appropriate in every type of writing. In which of the writings below might you find idioms used effectively? Circle your responses.

a fictional short story   a formal report   a personal letter

a business letter   a comic strip   movie dialogue

an instruction manual   a play   a scientific study report

Stating Idioms

Because idioms are culture-based, they eventually fall out of use as society changes. Many new idioms are added to the cultural language by young people. List below some of the idioms you use with your friends. Then put your list together with the lists of your classmates to create an extensive reference for use in your own writing.

1. _____

2. _____

3. _____

4. _____

5. _____

6. _____

7. _____

8. _____

Writing Tip

You can use an idiom reference book to add depth and subtlety to your writing. A good place to start is Houghton Mifflin's *The American Heritage Dictionary of Idioms* by Christine Ammer (1997).

 **Imagery**

Definition

Imagery: Words or phrases that appeal to the senses and conjure up mental images. Imagery helps readers imagine the sights, sounds, smells, tastes, and feelings associated with a character's or author's experiences. Imagery appears extensively in settings, character descriptions, and nature poetry.

Examples from Literature

Robert Louis Stevenson's *Treasure Island* begins with a vivid description of a sea-faring captain who enters an inn:

> I remember him as if it were yesterday, as he came plodding to the inn door, his sea-chest following behind him in a handbarrow; a tall, strong, heavy nut-brown man; his tarry pigtail falling over the shoulders of his soiled blue coat; his hands ragged and scarred, with black, broken nails; and the sabre cut across one cheek, a dirty, livid white. I remember him looking round the cove and whistling to himself as he did so, and then breaking out in that old sea-song that he sang so often after-ward....

The imagery in Clement Clarke Moore's "The Night Before Christmas" appeals to all the senses:

> The children were nestled all snug in their beds,
> While visions of sugar-plums danced in their heads;
> ...As dry leaves that before the wild hurricane fly,
> When they meet with an obstacle, mount to the sky.

The reader *feels* warmth; *tastes* and *sees* candy; *hears* and *smells* dry, crackling leaves; and *hears* and *feels* whistling winds.

Interpreting Imagery

You've probably seen many artistic representations of Santa Claus. On a separate piece of paper, draw one of your own based on Clement Clarke Moore's vivid imagery in "The Night Before Christmas." Compare your results with those of your classmates. Did all of you pick up on the same images to illustrate?

> He was dressed all in fur, from his head to his foot,
> And his clothes were all tarnished with ashes and soot;
> A bundle of toys he had flung on his back,
> And he looked like a peddler just opening his pack.
>
> His eyes—how they twinkled! his dimples how merry!
> His cheeks were like roses, his nose like a cherry;
> His droll little mouth was drawn up like a bow,
> And the beard on his chin was as white as the snow.
>
> The stump of a pipe he held tight in his teeth,
> And the smoke it encircled his head like a wreath;
> He had a broad face with a little round belly
> That shook, when he laughed, like a bowl full of jelly.
>
> He was chubby and plump—a right jolly old elf;
> And I laughed when I saw him, in spite of myself.

Using Imagery

Choose one of the experiences listed below, and write a detailed paragraph about it in the space provided. Do not name the experience you describe anywhere in your paragraph. Read your paragraph description to a classmate. Can your classmate guess which experience you described based on the images you used? Can your classmate feel, see, hear, taste, and smell the experience based on your description?

Experiences

studying in a quiet classroom

wandering through a zoo

riding a roller coaster

sitting beside a river

walking down a crowded city street

enjoying a summer day on the beach

Your Descriptive Paragraph:

_____

_____

_____

_____

_____

_____

_____

Reading Exercise

Read a nature poem and notice all the descriptive words and phrases it contains.

Writing Exercise

Bring a painting or photograph to life by writing a detailed description of the scene it portrays. Now try your hand at writing a descriptive poem that paints a picture of its own.

5 Metaphor and Simile

Definitions

Metaphor: A comparison that uses no connecting words. An *extended metaphor* carries the comparison throughout an entire work or section of a work.

Simile: A comparison between two seemingly unrelated things, using connecting words such as *like*, *as*, or *seems* in the comparison.

Examples from Literature

Li Po uses similes in these lines from "Taking Leave of a Friend":

> Mind like a floating wide cloud,
> Sunset like the parting of old acquaintances.

Carl Sandburg uses similes and metaphors to compare the sounds of a jazz band to winds moaning, cars speeding, and foes fighting in a stairwell in this passage from "Jazz Fantasia":

> Moan like an autumn wind high in the lonesome treetops…cry like a racing car slipping away from a motorcycle cop, bang-bang! you jazzmen, bang altogether drums, traps, banjoes, horns, tin cans—make two people fight on top of a stairway and scratch each other's eyes in a clinch tumbling down the stairs.

Emily Dickinson's comparison of the setting sun to a housewife extends throughout the poem "She Sweeps with Many-Colored Brooms," which begins:

> She sweeps with many-colored brooms,
> And leaves the shreds behind;
> Oh, housewife in the evening west,
> Come back, and dust the pond.

Locating Metaphors and Similes

Decide which two unlike things are being compared in the metaphors and similes below. Record your responses on the lines provided.

1. The groves were God's first temple.
   —William Cullen Bryant, "A Forest Hymn"

   _____ is compared to _____

2. O our Mother the Earth, O our Father the Sky.
   —Tewa Indian traditional poem, "Song of the Sky Loom"

   _____ is compared to _____

   _____ is compared to _____

3. I would not drop a single link / Of Memory's golden chain.
   —Sarah Josepha Hale, "Thirty-Five"

   _____ is/are compared to _____

4. …the long Minnesota winter shut down like the white lid of a box…the wind blew cold as misery.
   —F. Scott Fitzgerald, "Winter Dreams"

   _____ is/are compared to _____

   _____ is/are compared to _____

5. The movements of a rabbit are compared to what three things in this passage from D. H. Lawrence's Women in Love?

   And suddenly the rabbit, which had been crouching as if it were a flower, so still and soft, suddenly burst into life. Round and round the court it went, as if shot from a gun, round and round like a furry meteorite, in a tense hard circle that seemed to bind their brains.

   _____   _____   _____

Using Similes and Metaphors

A. Complete the following similes and metaphors. Decide whether each is a simile or a metaphor, and circle your decision.

  1. Life is like _____   simile   metaphor

  2. A dense forest seems like _____   simile   metaphor

  3. Memories act as _____   simile   metaphor

  4. Love is _____   simile   metaphor

  5. School is _____   simile   metaphor

  6. Pets are _____   simile   metaphor

B. Compare one of the topics from List One with one of the topics from List Two in an extended metaphor in a poem of your own.

List One	List Two
life	sailing
learning	nature
poetry	hiking
growing up	a movie
a dream	singing
family	a house
accomplishing a goal	playing sports

Writing Tip

Avoid *dead similes* and *metaphors,* which are those so overused they no longer contain much "punch" (e.g., "It cuts like a knife.").

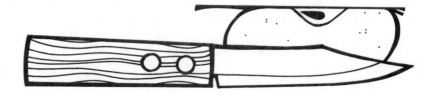

Oxymoron and Paradox

Definitions

Oxymoron: A two- or three-word phrase that contains opposite words or ideas. *Wise fool* is an oxymoron.

Paradox: An extended oxymoron. A paradox pits contradictory ideas against one another so that a statement appears to be untrue. However, when a reader evaluates a paradox in context, he or she discovers the paradox to hold a profound truth.

Examples from Literature

Shakespeare uses an oxymoron in act 2 of *Romeo and Juliet*: "Good night, good night! Parting is such *sweet sorrow.*"

John Milton's *Paradise Lost* demonstrates an oxymoron: "Yet from those flames no light, but rather *darkness visible.*"

Emily Dickinson's poem "There is a Solitude of Space" ends with an oxymoron: *"Finite Infinity."*

Notice the paradox in these two Emily Dickinson poem titles: "Much Madness is Divinest Sense" and "My Life Closed Twice Before Its Close."

In an essay on government, Ralph Waldo Emerson made his point with a paradoxical statement: "Good men must not obey the laws too well."

In "Death Be Not Proud" John Donne uses a paradoxical statement at the end of his poem to illustrate his belief in an afterlife:

> One short sleep past, we wake eternally
> And death shall be no more; *Death, thou shalt die.*

Defining Oxymorons

The complete meaning of an oxymoron is compacted into two or three words. On another piece of paper, write a full sentence explaining each of the following oxymorons.

1. working vacation
2. act normally
3. definite maybe
4. plastic glasses
5. found missing
6. small crowd

Interpreting Paradoxes

Many famous quotations contain paradoxes that state surprising truths. In two or three sentences, explain each of the following quotations.

1. Failure, in a sense, is the highway to success, insomuch as every discovery of what is false leads us to seek earnestly after what is true.
   —John Keats

2. A lie can travel halfway around the world while the truth is putting on its shoes.
   —Mark Twain

3. A lifetime of happiness! No man alive could bear it....
   —George Bernard Shaw, *Man and Superman* (1903), act 1

4. The wisest mind has something yet to learn.
   —George Santayana

5. I must be cruel only to be kind.
   —William Shakespeare, *Hamlet*, act 3 scene 4

6. What a pity that youth must be wasted on the young.
   —George Bernard Shaw

Creating Oxymorons

A. Match words from the first column with words from the second to create common oxymorons.

_____ 1. icy   a. estimate

_____ 2. bitter   b. sweet

_____ 3. jumbo   c. memory

_____ 4. exact   d. hot

_____ 5. forgettable   e. shrimp

B. Now create oxymorons of your own by adding opposite words or ideas to those presented here. For example: respectfully *disobedient*

1. bright   _____

2. truly   _____

3. completely   _____

4. large   _____

5. pretty   _____

Creating Paradoxes

Write paradoxical statements of your own to describe the nature of the following:

1. school _____

2. friendship _____

3. pets _____

4. family _____

5. movies _____

Reading Tip

Look for extended paradoxes in short stories and novels.

7 Personification

Definition

Personification: Giving human qualities or actions to something that is not human. Animals, inanimate objects, and ideas can all be personified. Personification appears frequently in both poetry and prose.

Examples from Literature

Personifying Animals

Fables and fairy tales often personify animals. In the Aesop's fable "The Mice in Council," the mice call a meeting, discuss plans, reject proposals, rise to their feet, sit in silence, and otherwise act like human beings.

Personifying Inanimate Objects

Stuffed animals are made to talk, feel, and behave as human beings in Margery Williams's *The Velveteen Rabbit.* Early in the story, nursery room magic that makes toys come to life is explained through a description of an old rocking horse. The description illustrates personification throughout:

> He was wise, for he had seen a long succession of mechanical toys arrive to boast and swagger, and by-and-by break their mainsprings and pass away, and he knew that they were only toys, and would never turn into anything else. For nursery magic is very strange and wonderful, and only those playthings that are old and wise and experienced like the Skin Horse understand all about it.

Personifying Ideas

Autumn turning into winter is personified in the O. Henry story entitled "The Cop and the Anthem." Changing weather patterns are even given a name ("Jack Frost"):

> A dead leaf fell in Soapy's lap. That was Jack Frost's card. Jack is kind to the regular denizens of Madison Square and gives them fair warning of his annual call.

Understanding and Identifying Personification

1. In the excerpt from *The Velveteen Rabbit,* it is suggested that mechanical toys will never turn into anything else. Still, the passage personifies the mechanical toys by suggesting they do three human things. The mechanical toys in this passage engage in what three human actions?

   _____

   _____

   _____

2. What is personified in this quote from William Shakespeare's *Macbeth*?

   Life's but a walking shadow, a poor player
   That struts and frets his hour upon the stage.

   Answer: _____

3. Underline all the examples of personification in this passage from Nathaniel Hawthorne's "Young Goodman Brown":

   He has taken a dreary road, darkened by all the gloomiest trees of the forest, which barely stood aside to let the narrow path creep through, and closed immediately behind.

4. Underline the ways in which grass is personified in this excerpt from the Emily Dickinson poem "The Grass so little has to do—":

   The Grass so little has to do—

   A sphere of simple Green—

   With only butterflies to brood

   And bees to entertain—

   And stir all day to pretty tunes

   The Breezes fetch along—

   And hold the sunshine in its lap

   And bow to everything—

Interpreting Personification

Many riddles are based on personification mixed with word plays. See if you can guess the answer to these riddles that rely on personification. Write your answers in the spaces provided.

1. What has eyes but cannot see? _____

2. What did one potato chip say to the other?

_____

3. How can you tell the difference between two types of trees?

_____

4. Why was the belt arrested?

_____

5. What does Mother Earth use to catch fish? _____

6. What do whales chew? _____

Using Personification

In a single phrase or sentence, personify each of the following by giving it human thoughts, feelings, attitudes, or actions. An example has been provided.

An abandoned house: *A sad and lonely house wept chipped paint onto the sidewalk.*

1. a lively young puppy: _____

2. freedom: _____

3. a busy shopping mall: _____

4. a firefly: _____

5. a mirror: _____

6. the sky: _____

Writing Exercise

Create a poem that personifies one of the above topics throughout the entire piece.

Symbol

Definition

Symbol: Something concrete that stands for something abstract. A symbol may be a person, place, thing, or action. It may stand for an idea, belief, feeling, or attitude.

A symbol keeps its own meaning while also standing for something else.

Examples from Literature

In "Mending Wall," Robert Frost describes the annual ritual of fixing a rock wall with his neighbor. In the poem, the wall symbolizes separation and the neighbor symbolizes unexamined tradition. The destruction and rebuilding of the wall are symbolic, too. The poem begins with the destruction of the wall:

> Something there is that doesn't love a wall
> That sends the frozen-ground-swell under it
> And spills the upper boulders in the sun,
> And makes gaps even two can pass abreast.

The word *something* symbolizes natural season changes. As the ground freezes, nature destroys the wall so two people can walk side by side. Nature doesn't like separation.

The poem continues with the rebuilding of the wall in the spring. The rebuilding symbolizes the human tendency to ignore nature and build barriers between one another.

> And on a day we meet to walk the line
> And we set the wall between us once again.
> And we keep the wall between us as we go.

When the narrator questions the need for the wall, his neighbor responds out of *darkness,* which symbolizes a thoughtless regard for tradition:

> He moves in darkness as it seems to me,
> Not of woods only and the shade of trees.
> He will not go behind his father's saying,
> And he likes having thought of it so well
> He says again, "Good fences make good neighbors."

Interpreting Symbols

Nathaniel Hawthorne uses a rose as a symbol in his story entitled "Dr. Heidegger's Experiment." Read passages from his story about a man who discovers the fountain of youth. Then decide what the rose symbolizes in the story.

> "This rose," said Dr. Heidegger, with a sigh, "this same withered and crumbling flower, blossomed five and fifty years ago. It was given to me by Sylvia Ward.... Five and fifty years it has been treasured between the leaves of this old volume. Now, would you deem it possible that this rose of half a century could ever bloom again?"
>
> He uncovered the vase, and threw the faded rose into the water which it contained.... The crushed and dried petals stirred...and there was the rose of half a century, looking as fresh as when Sylvia Ward had first given it to her lover.
>
> As they struggled to and fro, the table was overturned, and the vase dashed into a thousand pieces....
>
> "My poor Sylvia's rose...it seems to be fading again.... I love it well thus as in its dewy freshness," observed he, pressing the withered rose to his withered lips.

1. The rose probably symbolizes what in this story? _____

2. What does a rose symbolize in *Beauty and the Beast*? _____

3. Have you read any other stories or watched any movies that use a rose as a symbol? Can you make any generalizations about the symbolism associated with a rose based on those stories or movies? Explain below.

_____

_____

_____

_____

_____

_____

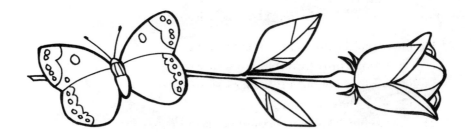

Considering Common Symbols

Some symbols become well known in a culture. Match the following common symbols with their meanings.

_____	1. a maple leaf	a. United States
_____	2. Uncle Sam	b. national pride
_____	3. a dove	c. poison
_____	4. a red rose	d. luck
_____	5. a skull and crossbones	e. youth
_____	6. springtime	f. life
_____	7. winter	g. love
_____	8. a path	h. peace
_____	9. a horseshoe	i. old age
_____	10. a nation's flag	j. Canada

Using Symbols

In a paragraph or two on another sheet of paper, describe the process of life using the following common symbols as defined above: a path, springtime, and winter.

Reading Tip

In literature, symbols are often complex. For example, the white whale in Herman Melville's *Moby Dick* takes on many meanings. Identify symbols in stories you read, and then look for their multiple meanings.

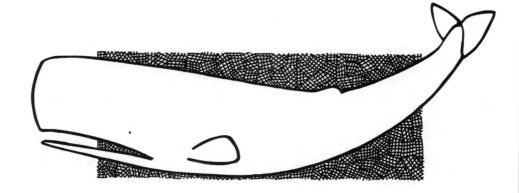

Alliteration

Definition

Alliteration: The repeating of beginning consonant sounds in a group of words. Alliteration refers to the first sound rather than the first letter. So "city slicker" is an example of alliteration, while *cake city* is not. Alliteration is common in slogans, clichés, and advertising because it emphasizes groups of words. It is common in poems because it adds a musical quality to the work.

Examples from Literature

Rudyard Kipling uses alliteration in these two citations from *The Jungle Book*:

> "I will go to the west wall," Kaa whispered.
> This is the hour of pride and power, / Talon and tusk and claw.

The tenth-century poem "The Ruin" uses alliteration to emphasize groups of words in this passage:

> Tumbled are the towers,
> Ruined the roofs,
> And broken the barred gate.

Shakespeare mocks the overuse of alliteration in this line from *A Midsummer Night's Dream*:

> Whereat, with blade, with bloody blameful blade,
> He bravely breached his boiling bloody breast.

Identifying Alliteration

1. The following Old English passage from *Beowulf* was written so long ago that it is hard to understand today. Still, the beautiful musical tone continues to please the ear thanks to the generous use of alliteration. Underline phrases within the passage that demonstrate alliteration.

> Now Beowulf bode in the burg of the Scyldings,
> leader beloved, and long he ruled
> in fame with all folk, since his father had gone
> away from the world, till awoke an heir,
> haughty Healfdene, who held through life,
> sage and sturdy, the Scyldings glad.
> Then, one after one, there woke to him,
> to the chieftain of clansmen, children four.

2. Underline the phrases that are emphasized by alliteration in these lines taken from throughout Edgar Allan Poe's "The Raven":

> Once upon a midnight dreary, while I pondered, weak and weary,...
> While I nodded, nearly napping, suddenly there came a tapping,...
> Doubting, dreaming dreams no mortal ever dared to dream before;...
> Open here I fling the shutter, when with many a flirt and flutter,...
> Nothing further then he uttered, not a feather then he fluttered—...
> Started at the stillness broken by reply so aptly spoken,...
> What this grim, ungainly, ghastly, gaunt, and ominous bird of yore...

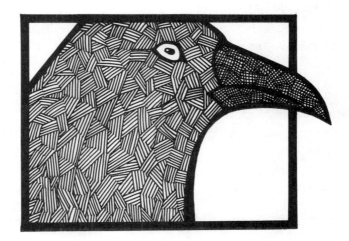

Using Alliteration

A. Revise the following sentences into ones that use alliteration. You may not change the mood or message of the sentence. You may change common nouns into proper nouns. A sample has been done for you.

> Hungry cows eat grass: *Cows craving cuisine crunch crops.*

1. A lonely person cries beside a body of water.

   _____

2. A funny girl cuts snowflakes out of cloth.

   _____

3. You shouldn't sleep when people who live near you are noisy.

   _____

4. A certain young man finds some sports boring.

   _____

5. My mother bakes great cupcakes.

   _____

B. Write a poem about yourself that uses alliteration based on the first letter in your name.

   _____

   _____

   _____

   _____

   _____

   _____

   _____

Assonance and Consonance

Definitions

Assonance: Repetition of vowel sounds at the beginning, middle, or end of a word.

Consonance: Repetition of consonant sounds anywhere within a word.

Examples from Literature

Assonance occurs at the beginning of words in this line from Robert Frost's "Mending Wall": "He is <u>a</u>ll pine, <u>a</u>nd I <u>a</u>pple orchard."

When assonance occurs in the middle of words as in this line from Edgar Allan Poe's "The Bells," it almost creates rhyme: "From the m<u>o</u>lten-g<u>o</u>lden n<u>o</u>tes."

This phrase from "The Hayloft" by Robert Louis Stevenson demonstrates that assonance relies on sounds, not letters themselves:

> Till the sh<u>i</u>ning sc<u>y</u>thes went far and w<u>i</u>de
> And cut it down to dr<u>y</u>.

The speech and descriptions of Kaa, the snake in Rudyard Kipling's *The Jungle Book*, are filled with s's to imitate hissing:

> "<u>S</u>o thi<u>s</u> i<u>s</u> the manling," <u>s</u>aid Kaa, "Very <u>s</u>oft i<u>s</u> hi<u>s s</u>kin, and he i<u>s</u> not <u>s</u>o unlike Banderlog."
> "<u>S</u>tay you <u>sssso</u>!" Kaa hi<u>ss</u>ed and the <u>c</u>ity wa<u>s s</u>ilent on<u>c</u>e more.

Consonance occurring at the end of words often creates near-rhymes as in this line from Walt Whitman's "I Saw in Louisiana a Live-Oak Growing":

> And its look ru<u>de</u>, unbending, lusty, ma<u>de</u> me think of myself.

Identifying Assonance

Underline the repeated vowel sounds in these lines from classic poems. Say the words aloud to help you hear repeating vowel sounds.

1. This is the ship of pearl, which poets feign (short i vowel sound)
    —Oliver Wendell Holmes, "The Chambered Nautilus"

2. I hear even now the infinite fierce chorus (long e vowel sound)
    —Henry Wadsworth Longfellow, "The Arsenal at Springfield"

3. On this green bank by the soft stream (long e vowel sound)
    —Ralph Waldo Emerson, "Concord Hymn"

4. Sleep sweetly in your humble graves (long e vowel sound)
    —Henry Timrod, "Ode on the Confederate Dead"

Identifying Consonance

Underline the repeated consonance sounds in these lines from classic poems.

1. Through the windows—through doors—burst like a ruthless force...
    (s sounds)
    —Walt Whitman, "Beat! Beat! Drums"

2. A soul admitted to itself / Finite Infinity (s and f sounds)
    —Emily Dickinson, "There is a Solitude of Space"

3. Lies stretching to my dazzled sight / A luminous belt, a misty light
    (s and l sounds)
    —John Greenleaf Whittier, "Hampton Beach"

4. And the poorest twig of the elm tree (t sounds)
    —James Russell Lowell, "The First Snowfall"

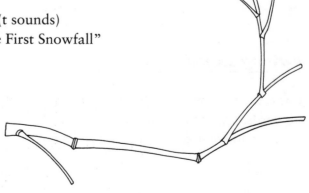

Distinguishing Assonance from Consonance

The following passages contain both assonance and consonance. Record below the words used to create each. A sample has been done for you.

> Beautiful glooms, soft dusks in the noonday fire—
> —Sidney Lanier, "The Marshes of Glynn"

Assonance: Beautiful, glooms, noonday
Consonance: glooms, soft, dusks

1. Who struck a streak with bad luck
   —Bret Harte, "The Outcast of Poker Flats"

   Assonance: _____

   Consonance: _____

2. Mother whose heart hung humble as a button
   —Stephen Crane, "War is Kind"

   Assonance: _____

   Consonance: _____

3. In silent night when rest I took
   —Anne Bradstreet, "Upon the Burning of Our House"

   Assonance: _____

   Consonance: _____

4. In Nothing and of Nothing all did build,...
   —Edward Taylor, Preface to "God's Determinations"

   Assonance: _____

   Consonance: _____

Writing Exercise

It is difficult to write with the intent of using assonance and consonance to emphasize groups of words, but often we do it naturally. Write a short poem. Then pick out the samples of assonance and consonance that occur in your piece.

Form

Definition

Form: The structure or shape of a written work. There are many forms of poetry. Some are highly structured and follow specific guidelines about syllables, rhymes, and rhythms. Other forms follow few or no specific rules.

Examples from Literature

The *haiku* is a Japanese poetry form that depicts everyday observations and simple life experiences. Japanese haikus are written in seventeen Japanese characters. Most English haikus consist of three lines in which the first line contains five syllables, the second seven syllables, and the third five syllables. Translations of Japanese haikus do not always follow English syllable requirements:

> Old pond
> Frog jumps in
> Splash!
> > —Matsuo Basho

> Under cherry trees
> Soup, the salad, fish and all
> Seasoned with petals.
> > —Matsuo Basho

The *cinquain* was first used by Adelaide Crapsey. It consists of five lines. The syllables of the lines follow the pattern 2–4–6–8–2:

> Listen
> With faint dry sound,
> Like steps of passing ghosts,
> The leaves, frost-crisp'd, break from the trees
> And fall.
> > —Adelaide Crapsey

Practicing Poetry

A. Try your hand at writing a cinquain, a haiku, and other poetry forms defined and illustrated here.

Your cinquain

_____

_____

_____

_____

_____

Your haiku

_____

_____

_____

B. The *limerick* is a funny poem that combines a couplet with a triplet. The first, second, and fifth lines rhyme. The third and fourth lines rhyme.

Sample from Mother Goose

There was an old man with a beard

Who said, "It is just as I feared!—

Two owls and a hen,

Four larks, and a wren,

Have all built their nests in my beard."

Your limerick

_____

_____

_____

_____

_____

C. *Skeltonic verse* was popularized by John Skelton. It is also known as "tumbling verse." It consists of short lines that continue a rhyme or near-rhyme for an indefinite number of lines until it flows into another rhyme or near-rhyme.

**Sample from John Skelton's
"To Mistress Margaret Hussey"**

With solace and gladness,

Much mirth and no madness,

All good and no badness;

So joyously

So maidenly,

So womanly.

Your Skeltonic verse

_____

_____

_____

_____

_____

_____

What's the Difference?

Identify each of the following poetry forms by writing a term listed below on each of the lines provided.

Poetry forms:

haiku · cinquain · Skeltonic verse · limerick

1. I know
   Not these my hands
   And yet I think there was
   A woman like me once had hands
   Like these.
   　　　　—Adelaide Crapsey

   Form: _____

2. The seed of all song
   Is the farmer's busy hum
   As he plants his rice.
   　　　　—Matsuo Basho

   Form: _____

3. There was a young lady whose chin
   Resembled the point of a pin:
   So she had it made sharp,
   And purchased a harp,
   And played several tunes with her chin.
   　　　　—Edward Lear

   Form: _____

4. As patient and as still
   and as full of good will
   As fair Isaphill
   Colyander
   Sweet pomander,
   Good Cassander;
   Steadfast of thought;
   Well made, well wrought
   Far may be sought
   Ere that ye can find
   So courteous, so kind
   　　　　—John Skelton

   Form: _____

Reading and Writing Exercise

Three more fun poetry forms are the *catalog poem*, which lists descriptions of its subject; the *picture poem*, which is written in lines that create an image; and *free verse*, which follows no prescribed form but concentrates instead on emotions. Locate and read samples of these poetry forms and try writing some of your own.

12 Onomatopoeia

Definition

Onomatopoeia: A word, such as *plop, buzz,* or *snap,* whose sound suggests its meaning. Onomatopoeia provides sound effects, and appears most frequently in poetry, advertising, and children's tales.

Examples from Literature

Alfred Lord Tennyson uses onomatopoeia in describing the sounds of birds and bees in these two lines from "The Princess":

> The *moan* of doves in immemorial elms,
> And *murmuring* of innumerable bees.

Edgar Allan Poe uses onomatopoeia to imitate the sound of bells in these lines from "The Bells":

> From the *jingling* and the *tingling* of the bells
> How they *clang*, and *crash*, and *roar*!

"Lepanto" by G. K. Chesterton illustrates onomatopoeia as well:

> Dim drums *throbbing*, in the hills half heard...
> Strong *gongs groaning* as the guns *boom* far.

Locating Onomatopoeia

Underline the samples of onomatopoeia in the lines and passages below:

1. Rattle-rattle, rattle-rattle,
   Bing!
   Boomlay, boomlay, boomlay, Boom,
   A roaring, epic, rag-time tune
   From the mouth of the Congo.
   　　　　—Vachel Lindsay, "The Congo"

2. ...let your trombones ooze, and go husha-
   husha-hush with the slippery sandpaper.
   　　　　—Carl Sandburg, "Jazz Fantasia"

3. Or roar of winds upon a wooded steep...
   The rushing of the sea-tides of the soul.
   　　　　—Henry Wadsworth Longfellow, "The Sound of the Sea"

4. Silver Bells!... How they tinkle, tinkle, tinkle.
   　　　　—Edgar Allan Poe, "The Bells"

5. So, as I stood, one blast of muttering thunder
   Burst in far peals along the waveless deep.
   　　　　—Percy Shelley, "Canto First"

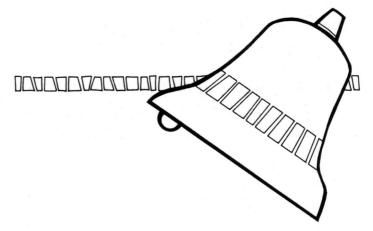

Hearing Onomatopoeia

A. Identify the onomatopoetic words associated with each of these sounds.

_____ 1. a tree branch breaking	a. bang, boom, crash
_____ 2. firecrackers exploding	b. plop, plop
_____ 3. a water faucet leaking	c. ring, ring
_____ 4. a telephone ringing	d. snap
_____ 5. a glass breaking	e. crash

B. Use onomatopoeia to describe the sounds of the following occurrences.

1. a mirror breaks _____

2. a door bell rings _____

3. a cymbal is struck _____

4. a woman screams _____

5. the wind blows gently _____

C. Write all the onomatopoetic words you can think of. Combine your list with those of your classmates to create a long class list that can be displayed for use in classroom writing.

_____	_____	_____
_____	_____	_____
_____	_____	_____
_____	_____	_____
_____	_____	_____
_____	_____	_____
_____	_____	_____
_____	_____	_____

Writing Exercise

Write a poem about all the sounds you hear in a place of your choice. Use as many onomatopoetic words as you can.

13 Parallelism

Definition

Parallelism: The repetition of words, phrases, or sentence structures. Parallelism adds rhythm and emotional impact to writing. It appears in poetry, speeches, and a variety of other literary forms.

Examples from Literature

This sentence from Rudyard Kipling's *The Jungle Book* repeats the noun in a series of clauses: "Kaa was everything the monkeys feared in the jungle, for <u>none</u> of them knew the limits to his power, <u>none</u> of them could look him in the face, and <u>none</u> had ever come alive out of his hug."

This stanza from the traditional Native American poem "Hunting Song" repeats prepositions and forms of the word *come*:

<u>From</u> the Mountain Black
<u>From</u> the summit,
Down the trail, <u>coming</u>, <u>coming</u> now
<u>Comes</u> the deer to my singing.

Thomas Jefferson repeats phrases beginning with the word *that* in this passage from the Declaration of Independence: "We hold these Truths to be self-evident, <u>that</u> all Men are created equal, <u>that</u> they are endowed by their Creator with certain unalienable Rights, <u>that</u> among these are Life, Liberty, and the pursuit of Happiness."

Parallelism is used throughout Lewis Carroll's "Jabberwocky" to create a musical quality, as demonstrated in these three lines:

"Beware the Jabberwock, my son!
The <u>jaws that bite</u>, the <u>claws that catch</u>!"

<u>One, two</u>! <u>One, two</u>! And <u>through</u> and <u>through</u>.

Locating Parallelism

Underline the parallelism in this excerpt from Chief Joseph's speech "I Will Fight No More Forever":

> I am tired of fighting. Our chiefs are killed. Looking Glass is dead. Toohoolhoolzote is dead. The old men are all dead. It is the young men who say yes and no. He who led on the young men is dead.

Underline the parallelism in this passage from Edgar Allan Poe's "A Predicament":

> The confusion and bustle in the streets were terrible. Men were talking. Women were screaming. Children were choking. Pigs were whistling. Carts they rattled. Bulls they bellowed. Cows they lowed. Horses they neighed. Cats they caterwauled. Dogs they danced.

Finding Mistakes in Parallelism

The following sentences contain errors in parallelism. Edit each to correct the errors. Write your corrected responses in the spaces provided. A sample has been done for you.

> Wrong: Mary likes to fish, hunt, camp, and swimming.
> Corrected: Mary likes to fish, hunt, camp, and swim.

1. Karla went to the store, bought bread, and she picked up some peanut butter and jelly.

   _____

2. Editing "Do's": Do check spelling. Do check grammar. Look for punctuation mistakes.

   _____

3. Kevin's hobbies include skiing, hiking, and he likes to read.

   _____

4. Daisuke walked into the room. He put his briefcase down. Pouring himself lemonade is what he did next. Then he relaxed in his favorite chair.

   _____

   _____

5. The dog ran past the red bench, around the spiky bushes, and through the river.

   _____

Categorizing Types of Parallelism

Decide what grammatical structure is repeated in these passages from American history. Indicate your answer by placing the appropriate letter beside each numbered passage.

Types of verb phrases

a. Verb phrases are repeated.
b. Sentences beginning with the same subject and verb are repeated.
c. A list of adjectives modify the same noun.
d. The sentence contains a series of prepositional phrases.
e. Repeated clauses contain the same subject and verb.

_____ 1. He has refused his assent to laws…. He has forbidden his Governors to pass laws…. He has refused to pass other laws….
—Thomas Jefferson, "The Declaration of Independence"

_____ 2. But in a larger sense, we cannot dedicate—we cannot consecrate—we cannot hallow—this ground.
—Abraham Lincoln, "The Gettysburg Address"

_____ 3. …that government of the people, by the people, for the people shall not perish from the earth.
—Abraham Lincoln, "The Gettysburg Address"

_____ 4. We the people of the United States, in order to form a more perfect union, establish justice, insure domestic tranquility, provide for the common defense, promote the general welfare, and secure the blessings of liberty to ourselves and our posterity, do ordain and establish this Constitution for the United States of America.
—Preamble to the Constitution of the United States

_____ 5. If I were in a monarchical government, or an autocratic or aristocratic government…
—Frederick Douglass, "Untie His Hands"

Writing Exercise

Try writing sentences that contain a series of prepositional phrases, clauses beginning with the same noun and verb, a series of -ing words, or a series of adjectives or adverbs.

Repetition and Refrain

Definitions

Repetition: Words or phrases repeated in writings to produce emphasis, rhythm, and/or a sense of urgency.

Refrain: The repetition of a word, phrase, line, or lines in a poem, song, or speech at regular intervals. Refrains often appear at the end of stanzas.

Examples from Literature

Edgar Allan Poe creates rhythm in his poem "The Bells," which is famous for its repetition that imitates the continual ringing of bells:

> To the swinging and the ringing
> of the bells, bells, bells—
> Of the bells, bells, bells, bells,
> Bells, bells, bells—
> To the rhyming and the chiming of the bells!

Stephen Crane uses repetition in both his prose and his poetry. In this passage from his short story, "The Open Boat," repetition appears in dialogue to suggest a sense of urgency: "'Bail her out, cook! Bail her out!' said the captain."

In his poem, "Do Not Weep Maiden, for War is Kind," Crane uses repetition and contrast for emphasis. After each stanza listing the horrors of war, the refrain "Do not weep. War is kind," is repeated to convince readers of the exact opposite.

Reasons for Repetition

Use context clues to help you decide why the authors chose to use repetition in the passages below. A sample passage from *Tom Sawyer* has been done for you.

> At this moment the crowd began to swag and struggle, and voices shouted, "It's him! It's him! He's coming himself!"
>   "Who? who?" from twenty voices.

Reason: Twain added both a rhythmic crowd-like sound and a sense of anticipation to this passage by using repetition in the murmurings of a crowd.

1. The folk song "Good Night, Irene" repeats a farewell in its refrain:

   > Irene, Good night. Irene, Good night.
   > Good night, Irene. Good night, Irene.
   > I'll see you in my dreams.

   Why might the refrain of this song contain repetition?

   _____

   _____

2. In "The American Crisis No. 1," Thomas Paine frequently repeats ideas in different words as illustrated in this passage: "…and as *I do not*, *I cannot* see on what grounds the king of Britain can look up to heaven for help against us…."

   Why might Paine repeat ideas in different words throughout his pamphlet?

   _____

   _____

3. The cook was a good cook, as cooks go; and as cooks go, she went.
       —Saki, "Reginald"

   Why is repetition useful in this humorous passage?

   _____

   _____

4. When a woman loses a necklace in Guy de Maupassant's "The Necklace," she tells her husband, "I…I…I…don't have Mme. Forestier's necklace."

   Why might the word *I* be repeated in this dialogue?

   _____

   _____

Hearing the Rhythm of Repetition

Sing these well-known American folk song refrains with your classmates to hear the rhythm created by repetition.

> Go tell Aunt Rhody, Go tell Aunt Rhody,
> Go tell Aunt Rhody, the old gray goose is dead.
>
> Swing low, sweet chariot, Comin' for to carry me home
> Swing low, sweet chariot, Comin' for to carry me home.
>
> Oh my darling, oh my darling, oh my darling Clementine
> You are lost and gone forever, oh my darling Clementine.
>
> She'll be comin' around the mountain when she comes
> She'll be comin' around the mountain when she comes
> She'll be comin' around the mountain, she'll be comin' around the mountain,
> She'll be comin' around the mountain when she comes.

Using Repetition

Use repetition to complete the following writing tasks on a separate sheet of paper.

1. Write a brief quote from a speech persuading people of the importance of voting.

2. Write a sentence or two of dialogue from a movie in which one character is urging another to quickly escape a burning building.

3. Create a short refrain to a song about school.

4. Write a two-lined refrain to a poem about love.

Reading Tip

Look for repetition in dialogue, poetry, and persuasive speeches. Take note of its effectiveness in creating rhythm, emphasis, and a sense of urgency.

15 Rhyme

Definition

Rhyme: The repetition of end sounds in words. *Perfect rhymes* repeat stressed vowel sounds and the last consonant sound. *Near rhymes* are two words that almost sound alike. Some near rhymes repeat stressed vowel sounds, but not the last consonant sound (i.e., home and bone). Others repeat end consonance, but not stressed vowels (i.e., home and same). *End rhymes* appear at the end of two or more lines of poetry. *Internal rhymes* appear within a single line of poetry. *Rhyme scheme* refers to the pattern of end rhymes in a poem.

Examples from Literature

This famous Mother Goose rhyme contains internal rhyme and end rhyme:

> Hark, *hark,* the dogs do *bark*!
> The beggars are coming to *town*
> Some in *rags* and some in *tags,*
> And one in a velvet *gown.*

The end rhyme in these two lines from "The Duel" by Eugene Field exemplifies a perfect rhyme:

> The gingham dog and the calico cat
> Side by side on the table sat.

The end rhyme in these two lines from Dante Rossetti's "The Blessed Damozel" exemplifies a near rhyme:

> From the gold bar of Heaven;
> Of waters still at even.

Identifying Ending Rhyme Patterns

Letters are used to identify a poem's rhyming pattern. The letter *a* is placed after the first line and all lines that rhyme with the first line. The letter *b* identifies the next line ending with a new sound, and all lines that rhyme with it. Letters continue to be assigned in sequence to lines containing new ending sounds. The following Mother Goose rhyme is said to have an *abba* rhyming pattern:

As I went to Bonner	*a*
I met a pig	*b*
Without a wig	*b*
Upon my word and honor.	*a*

Identify the rhyme pattern in each of the Mother Goose rhymes below by placing the correct letters after each line.

1. Cobbler, cobbler, mend my shoe. _____
   Get it done by half past two. _____

2. A cat came fiddling out of a barn, _____
   With a pair of bagpipes under arm. _____
   She could sing nothing but fiddle dee dee, _____
   The mouse has married the bumblebee. _____
   Pipe, cat; dance, mouse; _____
   We'll have a wedding at our house. _____

3. Bat, bat, come under my hat, _____
   And I'll give you a slice of bacon; _____
   And when I bake, _____
   I'll give you a cake, _____
   If I am not mistaken. _____

4. Dickery, dickery dare, _____
   The pig flew up in the air. _____
   The man in brown _____
   Soon brought him down, _____
   Dickery, dickery, dare. _____

5. Baa, baa, black sheep _____
   Have you any wool? _____
   Yes sir, yes sir, _____
   Three bags full. _____

6. Ring around the rosies, _____
   A pocket full of posies, _____
   Hush! Hush! Hush! _____
   All fall down. _____

Locating Internal Rhyme

Underline the words that create internal rhymes from these stanzas of Gelett Burgess's "An Alphabet of Famous Goops":

> Abednego was Meek and Mild; he Softly Spoke, he Sweetly Smiled.
> He never Called his Playmates Names, and he was Good in Running Games;
> But he was Often in Disgrace because he had a Dirty Face!
>
> Daniel and Dago were a Pair who Acted Kindly Everywhere;
> They studied Hard, as Good as Gold, they Always did as They were Told;
> They Never Put on Silly Airs, but They Took Things that were Not Theirs.
>
> When Festus was but Four Years Old his Parents Seldom had to Scold;
> They never Called him "Festus, Don't!" he Never Whined and said "I Won't!"
> Yet it was Sad to See him Dine. His Table Manners were Not Fine.

Writing Rhymes

In the space below, write a short poem using a rhyme scheme and rhyme types of your choice. Exchange papers with a classmate. Identify each other's rhyme schemes and types.

_____

_____

_____

_____

_____

_____

_____

_____

Writing Exercise

Try to make use of perfect rhymes, near rhymes, end rhymes, and internal rhymes all in one poem.

Rhythm

Definition

Rhythm: The pattern of beats or stresses in language. The pattern can be regular or random. Prose and free verse poetry display random patterns of beats. The regular patterns of stresses found in many poems and songs is called *meter*. Rhythm serves many purposes. It helps create mood by being fast or slow, calm or frenzied, for example. It can imitate action or emphasize a meaning or emotion. Rhythm is often combined with rhyme, alliteration, and other literary devices to add a musical quality to a work. Poetry scholars use symbols to indicate patterns of rhythm. The symbol (◡) indicates an unstressed syllable, and the symbol (/) indicates a stressed beat.

Examples from Literature

A common meter in classical English verse alternates stressed and unstressed syllables, as in the first line of William Cullen Bryant's "Thanatopsis":

> ◡ / ◡ / ◡ / ◡ / ◡ /
> To him who in the love of Nature holds

The rhythm of these lines from John Masefield's "Sea Fever" imitates rolling waves:

> I must go down to seas again, to the lovely sea and sky,
> And all I ask is a tall ship and a star to steer her by.

These lines from Rudyard Kipling's "Recessional" use rhyme, rhythm, consonance, assonance, and alliteration to create a musical quality:

> God of our fathers, known of old—
> Lord of our far-flung battle line—
> Beneath whose awful hand we hold
> Dominion over palm and pine.

Recognizing Regular Rhythms

The musical quality created by the rhythm in poetry is best appreciated when heard. Read each of the following stanzas aloud to get a feel for its rhythm. Then try to clap your hands to the beat of the poem. If you can clap out a clear beat, the poem has a regular meter. If you cannot clap easily to the beat of the poem, it demonstrates an irregular or random rhythm. After reading aloud and clapping, decide which poems demonstrate meter and which do not. Circle your responses.

1. There is no frigate like a book   meter   random rhythm
   To take us lands away,
   Nor any coursers like a page
   Of prancing poetry.
          —Emily Dickinson, "There Is No Frigate Like a Book"

2. The winter evening settles down   meter   random rhythm
   With smells of steaks in passageways
   Six o'clock.
   The burnt-out ends of smoky days.
          —T. S. Eliot, "Preludes"

3. Along the northern coast,   meter   random rhythm
   Just back from the rock-bound shore and the caves,
   In the saline air from the sea in Mendocino country,
          —Walt Whitman,
          "Song of the Redwood Tree," *Leaves of Grass*

4. Stand aside: the noise they make   meter   random rhythm
   Will cause Demetrius to awake.
          —William Shakespeare,
          A Midsummer Night's Dream

Writing Rhythm

A. Write a metered version of the free-verse poem below. Be certain your version discusses the same theme and uses some of the same words as the free-verse poem.

Free-verse version	Metered version
My living room,	_____
the day after Christmas:	_____
Ribbons, bows, paper, and tape	_____
lay separate from the boxes	_____
they clung to	_____
yesterday.	_____

B. Now write a free-verse version of the metered poem below.

Metered version	Free-verse version
In the classroom all alone	_____
After hours when we go home	_____
The janitor does sweep the floor	_____
And make our room look clean once more.	_____

Reading Exercise

Reading poetry aloud brings out the musical quality established by the rhythm, rhyme, and other poetic techniques. Read metered poems in unison with your classmates to help you identify rhythm patterns.

Writing Exercise

Many metered poems can be sung. Compose a tune for one of your favorite metered poems.

Run-on and End-stopped Lines

Definitions

End-stopped: The end of a line of poetry that coincides with the end of a thought. Commas, periods, semicolons, and colons often clue readers that a line is end-stopped. The reader should pause at an end-stopped line.

Run-on: Lines of poetry that continue forward in sense and punctuation into the next line. Reading on through run-on lines helps vary the rhythm of a poem.

Examples from Literature

Henry Wadsworth Longfellow's "The Tide Rises, the Tide Falls" contains both end-stopped and run-on lines:

end-stopped:	The tide rises, the tide falls,
end-stopped:	The twilight darkens, the curlew calls;
run-on:	Along the sea-sands damp and brown
end-stopped:	The traveller hastens toward the town,
end-stopped:	And the tide rises, the tide falls.

Context clues in Lewis Carroll's "Jabberwocky" help readers know where to pause and where to read on, even when the words themselves are unfamiliar. The reader is given two hints that the first line is a run-on line: it contains no end-mark, and the first word in the next line is a verb. The second line is an end-stopped line as indicated by the semicolon:

'Twas brillig, and the slithy toves
Did gyre and gimble in the wabe;
All mimsy were the borogoves,
And the mome raths outgrabe.

Distinguishing Between Poetry Line Types

Use context clues and end punctuation to help you decide whether each of the following lines from the first verse of the Negro National Anthem, "Lift Every Voice and Sing" by James Weldon Johnson, is an end-stopped or run-on line. Circle your responses.

1. Lift every voice and sing   end-stopped   run-on

2. Till earth and heaven ring,   end-stopped   run-on

3. Ring with the harmonies of Liberty;   end-stopped   run-on

4. Let our rejoicing rise   end-stopped   run-on

5. High as the listening skies,   end-stopped   run-on

6. Let it resound loud as the rolling sea.   end-stopped   run-on

7. Sing a song full of the faith that the dark past has taught us   end-stopped   run-on

8. Sing a song full of the hope that the present has brought us,   end-stopped   run-on

9. Facing the rising sun of our new day begun   end-stopped   run-on

10. Let us march on till victory is won.   end-stopped   run-on

Writing Run-on and End-stopped Lines

Choose one of the topics listed below. Then create a poem of your own using the line style pattern indicated.

Topics

school · farm life · the woods · the river · the ocean · city life · friends · parents
homework · movies · sports · poetry · music · art

_____ run-on

_____ end-stopped

_____ run-on

_____ end-stopped

_____ end-stopped

_____ end-stopped

_____ end-stopped

_____ end-stopped

_____ run-on

_____ run-on

_____ run-on

_____ end-stopped

_____ run-on

_____ end-stopped

_____ run-on

_____ end-stopped

Singing Tip

Next time you are singing a song, notice where the end-stopped and run-on lines are located. To hear the flow of rhythm created by run-on lines, do not take a break at the end of them.

18 Stanza

Definition

Stanza: A division in poetry equivalent to a paragraph in prose. Stanzas in most poetry forms follow a prescribed pattern of rhyme and rhythm. Free-verse poems follow no rules regarding where to divide stanzas. Common stanza patterns include couplets, triplets, quatrains, sestets, and octaves.

Examples from Literature

The stanzas in Joyce Kilmer's "Trees" are all couplets, including the first one:

> I think that I shall never see
> A poem lovely as a tree.

In the poem "Be Strong," Maltbie Davenport Babcock introduces each triplet stanza with a repetition of the poem's title:

> Be strong!
>
> We are not here to play, to dream, to drift
> We have hard work to do, and loads to lift;
> Shun not the struggle—face it; 'tis God's gift.

Many Mother Goose rhymes are written as one or more quatrains:

> All around the mulberry bush
> The monkey chased the weasel.
> The monkey thought 'twas all in fun.
> Pop! goes the weasel.

Interpreting Stanzas

Stanzas are named for the number of lines they contain:

couplet: 2 lines	**sestet:** 6 lines
triplet: 3 lines	**septet:** 7 lines
quatrain: 4 lines	**octave:** 8 lines
quintet: 5 lines	

Study the terms above and then identify the stanza style illustrated by each of the following stanzas.

1. Rain, rain, go away;
   Come again another day;
   Little Johnny wants to play.
   —Mother Goose

   stanza: _____

2. The rain is raining all around,
   It falls on field and tree
   It rains on the umbrellas here,
   And on the ships at sea.
   —Robert Louis Stevenson

   stanza: _____

3. Oh, Susan Blue,
   How do you do?
   Please may I go a walk with you?
   Where shall we go?
   Oh, I know—
   Down in the meadow where the
   cowslips grow!
   —Kate Greenaway

   stanza: _____

4. Said this little fairy,
   "I'm as thirsty as can be!"
   —Maud Burnham

   stanza: _____

5. On the grassy banks
   Lambkins at their pranks;
   Woolly sisters, woolly brothers
   Jumping off their feet
   While their woolly mothers
   Watch by them and bleat
   —Christina Rossetti

   stanza: _____

6. Over the river and through the
   woods,
   To grandfather's house we go;
   The horse knows the way
   To carry the sleigh
   Through the white and drifted
   snow.
   —Lydia Maria Child

   stanza: _____

Writing Poetry Stanzas

Read these sample stanzas from classic poems. Then try writing **stanzas of your own.**

> 1. Her air had a meaning, her movements a grace;
>   You turned from the fairest to gaze at her face.
>   —Elizabeth Barrett Browning, "My Kate"

Your couplet stanza:

_____

_____

> 2. O wild West Wind, thou breath of Autumn's being,
>   Thou, from whose unseen presence the leaves dead
>   Are driven, like ghosts from an enchanter fleeing.
>   —Percy Shelley, "Ode to the West Wind"

Your triplet stanza:

_____

_____

_____

> 3. Diddle, diddle, dumpling, my son John
>   Went to bed with his stockings on;
>   One shoe off and one shoe on,
>   Diddle, diddle, dumpling, my son John.

Your quatrain stanza:

_____

_____

_____

Reading and Writing Exercise

A sonnet begins with three quatrains and ends with a couplet. **Read some of Shakespeare's** famous sonnets, and then write one.

Allusion

Definition

Allusion: A reference made to a famous person, place, or event. Allusions can refer to historical events, geographic locations, Bible verses, mythology, poems, stories, characters, music, movies, plays, or art. Allusions conjure up complex images, ideas, or emotions in just a few words or phrases. Readers must recognize references for them to be effective, so allusions should be familiar to the author's intended audience.

Examples from Literature

Nathaniel Hawthorne makes a direct allusion when a character in "Dr. Heidegger's Experiment" says: "Did you never hear of the 'Fountain of Youth'…which Ponce de Leon, the Spanish adventurer, went in search of two or three centuries ago?"

Benjamin Franklin and Mark Twain used allusions humorously by adding new twists to old phrases and ideas. This passage from Franklin's *Poor Richard's Almanack* refers to a Bible verse: "Love your neighbor; yet don't pull down your hedge." In this passage from the same book he refers to mythological monsters that sported more than one head: "A mob's a monster; heads enough, but no brains."

Mark Twain twists a moral from Aesop's fables when he advises: "Put all your eggs in one basket, and—watch the basket." He alludes indirectly to the Bill of Rights when he says "It is by the goodness of God that in our country we have those three unspeakably precious things: freedom of speech, freedom of conscience, and the prudence never to practice either of them."

Interpreting Allusions

What thoughts, images, or ideas are conjured up by the allusions in italics in the sentences below?

1. The auto shop worker swept in like *Superman*, repaired my tire in a flash, and rescued me from the roadside.

   What does the allusion to Superman suggest?

   _____

2. Mary said, "Cale is my *Prince Charming!*"

   What does Mary think of Cale?

   _____

3. As more and more students joined in, the protest against the closing of our school's snack bar was beginning to look like a *March on Washington.*

   What can we tell about the protest by the allusion to a March on Washington?

   _____

4. Kevin doesn't do so well in math, but in art class, he's a regular *Picasso.*

   What can we tell about Kevin by the allusion to Picasso?

   _____

5. Brian, remember to leave your library book in the living room. If that book finds its way into the *black hole* in your bedroom, it will never find its way out!

   Do things often get lost in Brian's room? How do you know?

   _____

6. Every year, as we gazed on the pile of gifts under the tree, we knew Grandma had been our *Santa Claus* once again.

   Who bought the presents under the tree in this scenario? How do you know?

   _____

Appropriate Allusions

Match the allusions below with the scenes, events, or people they might best describe.

The scene, event, and people	The allusion

The scene, event, and people

_____ 1. the business district of a large city on Christmas morning

_____ 2. a generous woman

_____ 3. a great storyteller

_____ 4. the wedding of royalty and a commoner

_____ 5. a muscled teenager tears a car door off a wrecked car to save a man inside

The allusion

a. Hercules
b. Mark Twain
c. a ghost town
d. Mother Teresa
e. the story of Cinderella

Writing Allusions

Write a paragraph about one of the allusions listed above and its matching scene, event, or people. Be certain to mention the allusion in your paragraph and include enough details to develop the comparison.

Reading Exercise

Classic stories often allude to Shakespeare, the Bible, or mythology. When you run into unfamiliar allusions, look them up on the Internet or in an allusion dictionary such as *The Wordsworth Dictionary of Classical and Literary Allusion* by A. H. Lass.

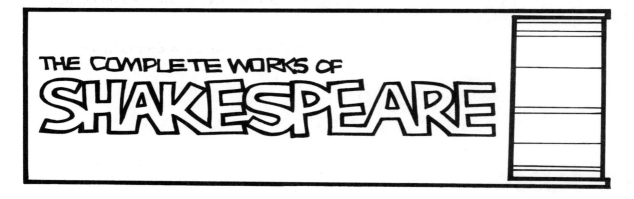

Characters and Characterization

Definitions

Characters: The people or animals in short stories, novels, and plays. The *protagonist* is the central character. The *antagonist* is his opponent. *Major* characters include the protagonist, the antagonist, and other characters who have a large role in the story. *Minor* characters have a smaller role in the story. *Flat* characters have only one or two sides. *Round* characters have many sides. *Static* characters experience no major change in the story. *Dynamic* characters change, grow, or learn something by the end of the story.

Characterization: The ways in which an author reveals the traits of characters to his audience. *Direct* characterization is a method wherein the author tells his readers about a character. *Indirect* characterization methods require the reader to infer facts about a character's traits. Indirect methods of characterization include the actions and words of a character; a physical description of a character; the thoughts of a character; and the thoughts, actions, and words of other characters.

Example from Literature

Superheroes are flat, static protagonists. They display only a good side and experience no growth or personality changes during their adventures.

The beast in *Beauty and the Beast* is a round, dynamic protagonist. He can be kind or cruel, selfish or giving, brave or afraid, depending on the circumstances. By the end of the story, his attitude and behavior changes reflect a new understanding of compassion.

Kinds of Characters

Circle the word that best describes the following characters.

1. Scrooge   static   dynamic

2. Superman   flat   round

3. The Little Mermaid   static   dynamic

4. Cinderella's stepmother   flat   round

5. Tom Sawyer   flat   round

Characterization Methods

What method is used to develop characters in the following passages from Robert Louis Stevenson's *Treasure Island*? Indicate your response by placing a letter from the key in each of the blanks.

Characterization Methods

a. The author directly tells the reader about the character.
b. The character's physical appearance is described.
c. The characters thoughts, actions, or words are recorded.
d. The thoughts, actions, or words of another character reveal something about the character being developed.

_____ 1. All the crew respected and even obeyed him. He had a way of talking to each, and doing everybody some particular service. (spoken by the story's protagonist)

_____ 2. He was a very silent man by custom. (stated as part of the narration)

_____ 3. When I got back with the basin, the doctor had already ripped up the captain's sleeve, and exposed his great sinewy arm. It was tattooed in several places.

_____ 4. But he broke in cursing the doctor, in a feeble voice, but heartily. "Doctors is all swabs," he said; "and that doctor there, why, what do he know about seafaring men?"

Creating Characters

On another sheet of paper, answer the following questions about a protagonist you might create. Then use the various forms of characterization to reveal that character to readers in a brief description.

1. Describe your character's physical characteristics.
2. What is your character's greatest ambition?
3. What is your character's greatest fear?
4. Who does your character love more than anyone?
5. Describe your character's overall personality.
6. What are your character's talents and hobbies?
7. What are your character's flaws?
8. Who are your character's friends?
9. Who are your character's enemies?
10. What does your character cherish and respect?
11. What does your character despise and fight against?
12. How does your character relate to other people?

Writing Exercise

Answer the above questions for an antagonist. Then create a story involving the protagonist and antagonist you created.

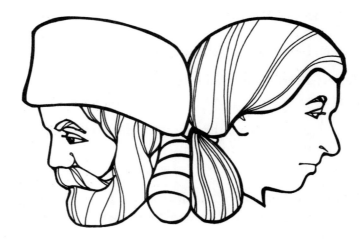

21 Conflict

Definition

Conflict: **A struggle between two opposing forces in a novel, short story, or play. A story's plot is developed around one or more of five basic conflicts: character versus character, character versus nature, character versus society, character versus fate, character versus self.**

Examples from Literature

"The Three Little Pigs" pits characters against character—the pigs against the wolf.

Charlotte's Web by E. B. White pits characters against fate as Charlotte, the spider, saves Wilbur, the pig, from slaughter.

Gary Paulsen's *Hatchet* pits a young boy against nature when he finds himself to be the sole survivor of a plane crash that lands him in the wilderness.

Mark Twain's Tom Sawyer is pitted against society in his adventures as he tries to live outside of the rules of his aunt and his community.

One of the conflicts Meg experiences in Madeleine L'Engle's *Wrinkle in Time* occurs within herself when she has to decide what to believe about her father, her adventures, and herself.

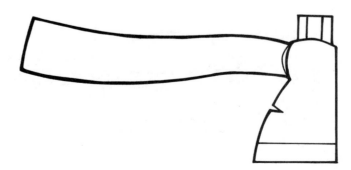

Classifying Conflicts

Which type of conflict is represented by each of the movie summaries presented here? Indicate your response by placing the appropriate letter beside each number. Some letters will be used more than once.

Types of Conflict

a. character vs. character
b. character vs. nature
c. character vs. fate
d. character vs. self (internal conflict)
e. character vs. society

_____ 1. In *Toy Story*, Buzz and Woody experience a personality clash.

_____ 2. Mike and Sulley go against the practices of the entire Monster race when they befriend a child in *Monsters, Inc.*

_____ 3. Chickens in *Chicken Run* attempt to beat their fate of being turned into chicken pot pies.

_____ 4. A teenage boy in *A Cry in the Wild* crash-lands a plane in the Canadian wilderness.

_____ 5. In *Big Daddy*, a young man must look within himself to decide whether he can raise a child who appears on his doorstep.

_____ 6. A team of Jamaican athletes must fight against an Olympic committee and a common belief held by their own people to become their country's first bobsled team in *Cool Runnings*.

_____ 7. In *Home Alone*, a young boy takes on would-be robbers who enter his house.

_____ 8. A lawyer is conflicted within himself about telling the truth in his business practices and personal life in the movie *Liar, Liar.*

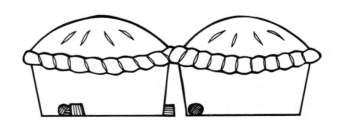

Creating Conflicts

Choose one or two characters and a setting from the lists below. Then write a possible conflict to fit each type presented. A sample has been done for you.

Characters		Settings	
horse	teacher	city	farm
cow	student	campground	stadium
parent	old man	classroom	Hawai'i
child	poor woman	another planet	grocery store
farmer	alien		

Sample: Character vs. character conflict
A cow and a horse fight to become their farmer's favorite pet.

1. Character vs. character conflict:

   _____

2. Character vs. nature conflict:

   _____

3. Character vs. fate conflict:

   _____

4. Character vs. society conflict:

   _____

5. Character vs. self conflict:

   _____

Writing Exercise

Develop one of your conflicts into a complete short story.

Reading Exercise

Most stories include several minor conflicts alongside the plot's major conflict. Identify all the minor conflicts in the next story you read in literature class.

Dialect

Definition

Dialect: An author's use of speech patterns that fit a character's background. Dialect differs in its details of vocabulary, grammar, pronunciation, and expression. It gives hints about a character's regional, educational, social, economic, and historical background. Dialect helps to make a character and setting appear realistic.

Examples from Literature

The first line of Mark Twain's *Adventures of Huckleberry Finn* illustrates the speech patterns of lower-class Mississippi Valley residents in the late nineteenth century:

> You don't know about me without you have read a book by the name of *The Adventures of Tom Sawyer*; but that ain't no matter.

William Shakespeare's characters speak in Old English as in this line spoken by Leonato from *Much Ado About Nothing:*

> How now, brother, where is my cousin, your son?
> Hath he provided this music?

Sir Thomas Malory's work contains the Medieval dialect of Romanticism: "And thus it past on from Candylmas untyl after Ester that the moneth of May was com, whan every lusty harte begynneth to blossom and burgyne."

Many of Bret Harte's characters speak in the dialect of the Old West, as demonstrated in this line from *Captain Jim's Friend*: "Well, the hull thing'll be settled now, boys; Lacy Bassett is coming down yer to look round...."

Interpreting Dialect

A. Restate these passages from the previous page in standard English.

1. You don't know about me without you have read a book by the name of *The Adventures of Tom Sawyer*; but that ain't no matter.

   _____

   _____

2. How now, brother, where is my cousin, your son? / Hath he provided this music?

   _____

3. And thus it past on from Candylmas untyl after Ester that the moneth of May was com, whan every lusty harte begynneth to blossom and burgyne.

   _____

   _____

4. Well, the hull thing'll be settled now, boys; Lacy Bassett is coming down yer to look round.

   _____

   _____

B. On another sheet of paper, try your hand at the following passages too.

1. As fair art thou, my bonnie lass,
   So deep in luve am I;
   And I will luve thee still, my dear,
   Till a' the seas gang dry.
   —Robert Burns, "Red, Red Rose" (written in Scottish dialect)

2. "Well," Smiley says, easy and careless, "he's good enough for *one* thing, I should judge—he can outjump any frog in Calaveras County."
   —Mark Twain, "The Celebrated Jumping Frog of Calaveras County"
   (written in the dialect of the Mississippi Valley in the late nineteenth century)

Identifying Dialect

Match the following words and phrases with their region, time period, or social group.

_____ 1. feller   a. modern teenagers

_____ 2. chillin'   b. eighteenth-century Quakers

_____ 3. sire   c. the Old West

_____ 4. thee   d. Medieval times

_____ 5. peace   e. the sixties

Unscrambling Dialect

Name these two familiar songs that have been written in unfamiliar dialects.

1. At the summit of a platter full of pasta enveloped in parmesan, I misplaced my distressed sphere of beef when an individual responded to an allergic trigger with a nasal scream.

   Name the song _____

2. Flash, flash, miniature sky rock.
   Where are you, man? Out of this world,
   Like a sky diamond.
   Flash, flash, miniature sky rock.
   Where are you, man?

   Name the song _____

Writing Exercise

Practice writing dialect by translating a single sentence into words that might be used by various people—from aliens to cowboys, to pioneers and rap singers.

23 Dialogue

Definition

Dialogue: Conversation between two or more characters. Plays are comprised almost entirely of dialogue. Dialogue appears more frequently in modern fiction than in older works. Dialogue can move the action of a story, build suspense, arouse reader interest, develop characters, add variety, establish conflict, and make a story's characters and setting seem real.

Examples from Literature

Characters in Sherlock Holmes stories frequently tell the detective (and the reader) about past actions using dialogue. A client in "The Yellow Face" tells the detective:

> "Still plucking at my sleeve she led me away from the cottage. As we went I glanced back, and there was the yellow, livid face watching us out of the upper window."
> —Sir Arthur Conan Doyle, *The Memoirs of Sherlock Holmes*

Dialogue helps set the scene, identify characters, and reveal emotions in this interaction between a father and his daughters from James Whitcomb Riley's "At Last":

> The father turns; a sharp, swift flash of pain flits over his face: "Amanda, child! I said a moment since—I see I must *again*—Go take your little sisters off to bed! There, Effie, Rose, and *Clara mustn't cry*!"
> "I tan't he'p it—I'm fyaid 'at mama'll die!"

Identifying the Purpose of Dialogue

Identify the purpose of the dialogue used in the following passages from Beatrix Potter stories. Indicate your responses by placing a letter from the key beside each number. Note that some letters may be used more than once, and some dialogue samples may have more than one purpose.

Purpose of Dialogue

a. This dialogue helps describe a character.
b. This dialogue builds suspense.
c. This dialogue creates a fast pace.
d. This dialogue helps transition from one action to another.
e. This dialogue sets a mood.

_____ 1. "Whatever is the matter, Cousin Benjamin? Is it a cat? Or John Stoat Ferret?"

"No, no, no! He's bagged my family—Tommy Brock—in a sack—have you seen him?"

"Tommy Brock? How many, Cousin Benjamin?"

"Seven, Cousin Peter, and all of them twins! Did he come this way? Please tell me quick!"

—*The Tale of Mr. Tod*

_____ 2. "Come in, Cousin Ribby, come in and sit ye down! I'm in sad trouble, Cousin Ribby," said Tabitha, shedding tears.

—*The Roly-Poly Pudding*

_____ 3. "Now, my dears," said old Mrs. Rabbit one morning, "you may go into the fields or down the lane, but don't go into Mr. McGregor's garden: your Father had an accident there; he was put in a pie by Mrs. McGregor."

—*The Tale of Peter Rabbit*

_____ 4. "Now run along, and don't get into mischief. I'm going out."

—*The Tale of Peter Rabbit*

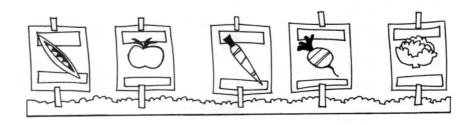

Writing Dialogue

On another sheet of paper, convert the following two scenes into dialogue.

1. A boy and girl are walking to school one morning. The boy realizes he has forgotten an important schoolbook. He wants to go back and get it before proceeding on to school. The girl doesn't want to go back for the book because she is afraid they will be late for school.

    (Write the debate they have about whether or not to go back for the book.)

2. Christmas morning at the Baker home starts out sad. Mr. Baker recently lost his job and there are few presents under the tree. Four-year-old Tommy Baker wakes up last. He walks into the living room and says something that makes the rest of his family smile. A happy conversation follows.

    (What did Tommy say? What conversation followed?)

Reading Exercise

Select a short story with lots of dialogue. Read only the dialogue in the story. Does the story make sense when you read just the dialogue? Now read the story without the dialogue. Does the story make sense without the dialogue? What does dialogue add to a story? Why are the other parts of the story necessary, too?

Flashback

Definition

Flashback: An interruption in a story to tell about events that happened earlier. Flashbacks can appear as character memories or dreams, or in dialogue or narration. Flashbacks provide background information that clarifies current actions in the story.

Examples from Literature

A flashback appears as the memory of the character of the banker in Anton Chekhov's "The Bet":

> And now the banker, walking to and fro, remembered all this, and asked himself: "What was the object of that bet?"

Sherwood Anderson moves right into a flashback in the narrative of his short story "Sophistication":

> Always he had been conscious of the girl growing into womanhood as he grew into manhood. Once, on a summer night when he was eighteen, he had walked with her on a country road and in her presence had given way to an impulse to boast, to make himself appear big and significant in her eyes.

A flashback about steering a riverboat through a difficult spot in the river is related through dialogue in Mark Twain's *Life on the Mississippi:*

> "Jim, how did you run Plum Point, coming up?"
>   "It was in the night there, and I ran it the way one of the boys on the *Diana* told me...."

Why Flash Back?

On another sheet of paper, answer the following questions:

1. What are some of the reasons an author might choose to use flashbacks instead of beginning at the start of a story and telling it chronologically?

2. What are some of the ways flashbacks are accomplished in novels and short stories? How are they accomplished in movies and plays?

3. Have you ever read or viewed a flashback that was more confusing than effective? Describe the flashback. Why was it confusing? How could it have been presented more effectively?

Find the Flashback

Underline the flashback section of the following passage from Sherwood Anderson's "The Teacher."

Snow lay deep in the streets of Winesburg.... Young George Willard, who had nothing to do, was glad because he did not feel like working that day. The weekly paper had been printed and taken to the post office Wednesday evening and the snow began to fall on Thursday. At eight o'clock, after the morning train had passed, he put a pair of skates in his pocket and went up to Waterworks Pond but did not go skating. Past the pond and along a path that followed Wine Creek he went until he came to a grove of beech trees. There he built a fire against the side of a log and sat down at the end of the log to think. When the snow began to fall and the wind to blow he hurried about getting fuel for the fire.

The young reporter was thinking of Kate Swift.... On the evening before he had gone to her house to get a book she wanted him to read and had been alone with her for an hour. For the fourth or fifth time the woman had talked to him with great earnestness and he could not make out what she meant by her talk. He began to believe she must be in love with him and the thought was both pleasing and annoying.

Up from his log he sprang to pile sticks on the fire. Looking about to be sure he was alone he talked aloud pretending he was in the presence of the woman.

Writing a Flashback

Try your hand at writing a flashback by completing a story using the transitions provided.

Forgive me. It is not a story that lends itself to the telling from beginning to end, from top to bottom. Rather, I begin somewhere in the middle. _____

_____

_____

_____

The whole thing started when _____

_____

_____

_____

So that brings us up to this afternoon. _____

_____

_____

_____

Foreshadowing

Definition

Foreshadowing: Hints about events that will occur further on in a story. Hints may appear in dialogue or narration. Foreshadowing is used to develop plots, set a mood of intrigue and suspense, and prepare the reader for what is to come.

Examples from Literature

An orphan learns his true identity and claims his inheritance in Charles Dickens's *Oliver Twist*. Many hints along the way foreshadow this outcome. For example, when Oliver sees a photograph of a woman who he later learns is his deceased mother, he gets the feeling the picture wants to speak to him. And when Oliver's grandfather meets Oliver for the first time, the old man recognizes a familiarity of features.

Even the title of Paul Laurence Dunbar's "The Scapegoat" hints that the protagonist is going to take a fall. Descriptions of the ambitions of Mr. Asbury further the foreshadowing. "Now so much success must have satisfied any other man," Dunbar writes, suggesting that Mr. Asbury is going to go too far. Again the reader is made uneasy about future events when he is told, "It was against the advice of his friends that [Asbury] asked for admission to the bar." Yet when Asbury does meet his demise, the story is only half over, and the foreshadowing leads in another direction. It becomes clear the scapegoat is going to do some scapegoating of his own when his old political enemy comes to visit. Bingo is sure that Asbury has lost all political power and drive, but "he did not see the gleam in Asbury's half-shut eye."

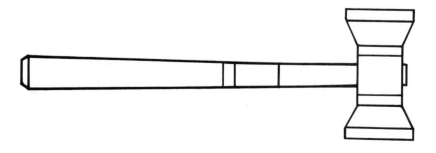

Foreshadowing in Fairy Tales

Fairy tales often use blatant hints and repetition to build suspense and foreshadow future events. In complete sentences, answer these questions about foreshadowing in fairy tales.

1. What changes in the attitudes and actions of the title characters of *Beauty and the Beast* foreshadow their falling in love?

   _____

   _____

2. What clues should Little Red Riding Hood have recognized to realize that her grandmother was not really her grandmother?

   _____

   _____

3. How does the reader know that Goldilocks is going to be discovered by the bear family in "The Three Little Bears"?

   _____

   _____

4. Recall the story of "The Three Little Pigs." How does the reader know the wolf is going to arrive at the brick house after visiting the house of twigs? Why is the reader not surprised that the wolf cannot blow down the house of bricks as he has the houses made of straw and twigs?

   _____

   _____

5. Why is the reader not surprised when a carriage turns into a pumpkin and a dress into rags in "Cinderella"?

   _____

   _____

Rewriting "The Ugly Duckling"

Hans Christian Andersen uses foreshadowing in "The Ugly Duckling" to hint that the title character is a swan. Review five of the main hints from his famous story:

1. The ugly duckling's egg is larger than the rest, its shell is harder, and it takes longer to hatch.

2. When another character in the story suggests the ugly duckling may be a turkey, the mother responds: "Oh, that is not a turkey; how well he uses his legs, and how upright he holds himself."

3. When the mother watches the ugly duckling swim, she comments, "[He] swims as well or even better than the others. I think he will grow up pretty."

4. When the ugly duckling runs into a flock of swans, the narrator tells us, "As they mounted higher and higher in the air, the ugly little duckling felt quite a strange sensation as he watched them.... He...stretched out his neck towards them, and uttered a cry so strange that it frightened himself.... He felt towards them as he had never felt for any other bird in the world."

5. After the ugly duckling spends a winter alone, he returns to a pond. "Then he flew to the water, and swam towards the beautiful swans. The moment they espied the stranger, they rushed to meet him with outstretched wings."

On a separate piece of paper, rewrite the story, revealing at the end of your version that the ugly duckling is something other than a swan. Use foreshadowing in both your dialogue and narration to hint that your ugly duckling is an alien, a robot, a goose, or anything else of your choice.

Reading Tip

When reading a mystery book, look for elements of foreshadowing that help you solve the mystery before you reach the end of the story.

Genre

Definition

Genre: A category of literature. The four major literary genres are nonfiction prose, fiction prose, poetry, and drama. More specific genres include mysteries, science fiction, epic poems, melodramas, historical fiction, essays, realistic fiction, persuasive speeches, and comic dramas. Considering an entire work and its purpose helps readers identify genre. Hints within a work point to its genre, as well. For example, alien characters in a story alert the reader that the tale fits into the science fiction genre. A story set in the Civil War is likely a piece of historical fiction.

Examples from Literature

Although authors sometimes cross over, many become famous for works of certain genres. Many Mark Twain stories fall into the genre of historical fiction, for example. Shakespeare is famous for sonnets, and tragic and comic dramas. Sir Arthur Conan Doyle is known for his Sherlock Holmes mysteries.

Characters, settings, dialogue, and narration can all give hints as to a work's genre. The fanciful creatures in J. R. R. Tolkien's *The Hobbit* suggest the work is a fantasy. This narration from Mary Shelley's *Frankenstein* hints that the work is a horror story: "I passed the night wretchedly. Sometimes my pulse beat so quickly and hardly that I felt the palpitation of every artery; at others, I nearly sank to the ground through languor and extreme weakness."

Categorizing Genres

Place the specific genres under the major genre categories to which they belong.

Specific Genres

essay	biography	comedy	screenplay	lyric
letter	historical fiction	epic	melodrama	mystery
horror	persuasive speech	farce	nature poem	sonnet
report	science fiction	fantasy	free verse	tragedy

Nonfiction prose	Fiction prose	Poetry	Drama
_____	_____	_____	_____
_____	_____	_____	_____
_____	_____	_____	_____
_____	_____	_____	_____
_____	_____	_____	_____

Identifying Genres

Name the specific genre of each work listed below. Choose from the following: sonnet, fantasy, biography, persuasive speech, report, and farce.

1. The movie *Austin Powers* _____

2. *Goosebumps* tales _____

3. Dr. Martin Luther King's "I Have a Dream" speech _____

4. Lewis Carroll's *Alice in Wonderland* _____

Using Genres Effectively

Name the specific genre you would use to accomplish the following goals:

1. Persuade readers to use solar power at their homes _____

2. Describe the lifestyle of ordinary people in the 1800s _____

3. Tell the story of an alien and a talking dog _____

Matching Genres

Clues in dialogue and narration alert readers to genres. Use context clues to help you match each classic passage with its genre.

Genres

a. mystery   e. fantasy
b. lyric poem   f. drama
c. horror   g. essay
d. historical fiction

_____ 1. Milo's eyes opened wide, for there in front of him was a large dog with a perfectly normal head, four feet, and a tail—and the body of a loudly ticking clock.
—Norton Juster, *The Phantom Tollbooth*

_____ 2. What is an epigram? A dwarfish whole / It's body brevity, and wit its soul.
—Samuel Taylor Coleridge

_____ 3. Act 1, scene 1, Elsinore. A platform before the castle.
Enter Bernardo and Francisco, two sentinels.
Bernardo. Who's there?
—William Shakespeare, *Hamlet*

_____ 4. I trembled excessively; I could not endure to think of...the occurrences of the preceding night.
—Mary Shelley, *Frankenstein*

_____ 5. "We opened every possible drawer; and I presume you know that, to a properly trained police agent, such a thing as a *secret drawer* is impossible."
—Edgar Allan Poe, *The Purloined Letter*

_____ 6. The schoolmaster, always severe, grew severer and more exacting than ever.
—Mark Twain, *The Adventures of Tom Sawyer*

_____ 7. Nothing is at last sacred but the integrity of your own mind. Absolve you to yourself.
—Ralph Waldo Emerson, "Self-Reliance"

Writing Exercise

Try to convert a single theme to numerous genres. How do they differ?

Irony

Definition

Irony: A contradictory statement or situation. *Verbal irony* occurs when a character says one thing but means the opposite. In drama, verbal irony is often accompanied by an ironic tone of voice and ironic expressions. *Situational irony* occurs when what happens in a story is the opposite of what is expected to happen. *Dramatic irony* occurs when the reader has information that one or more of the characters does not have.

Examples from Literature

Verbal Irony

The antagonist in Richard Connell's "The Most Dangerous Game" kidnaps and then hunts people. When he says, "We'll visit my training school.... It's in the cellar. I have about a dozen pupils down there now," he is not referring to pupils and a school, but to captives and a prison.

Situational Irony

The protagonist in Guy de Maupassant's "The Necklace" works for years to replace an expensive necklace she borrowed and lost only to learn in the end that the necklace was a fake. That plot exemplifies situational irony.

Dramatic Irony

Shakespeare's *As You Like It* is a story of mistaken identity in which the audience is aware of the true identities of the players involved, but the characters are often confused by disguises. This is an example of dramatic irony.

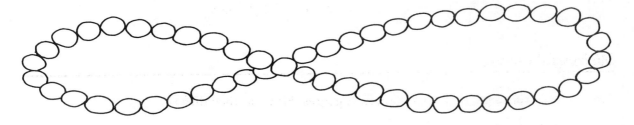

Understanding Irony

1. The antagonist in "The Most Dangerous Game" brags that he hunts the most dangerous animal of all. What is ironic about this claim?

   _____

   _____

2. What is ironic about the ending of "The Necklace"?

   _____

   _____

3. Explain irony in your own words.

   _____

   _____

4. Give an example of dramatic irony from a movie you have watched.

   _____

   _____

Predicting Irony

1. Hans Christian Andersen wrote a famous story about a family of ducks who make fun of a young waterfowl for his ugliness. What irony reveals itself at the end of "The Ugly Duckling"?

   _____

   _____

2. O. Henry was a master of surprise endings. In one story, called "The Cop and the Anthem," he tells of a homeless man who makes numerous attempts to get arrested so he can spend the cold winter months in a warm jail cell. After all of his attempts fail to get him arrested, he stops beside a church where he stands listening to a choir sing. The beautiful music inspires the homeless man to get a job and straighten out his life. He no longer wishes to spend the winter in jail. Predict the ironic ending to this O. Henry classic.

   _____

   _____

Identifying Irony

1. Your friend asks how you did on your spelling test. You failed, but respond "Marvelously." Your response is an example of which type of irony?

   _____

2. You buy a pizza at full price after looking all over the house and not finding your five-dollars-off coupon. You return home with the pizza and grab a paper plate out of the cupboard. Just as you are about to place a slice of pizza on the plate, you notice a piece of paper on top of the plate. The piece of paper is the coupon you couldn't find. This scenario is an example of which type of irony?

   _____

3. You are watching a scene in a movie. The shot shows a split screen on which the viewer can see two characters talking to each other on the phone. The characters, of course, cannot see each other, and have somehow mistaken each others' voices for those of other characters in the movie. This mistaken identity confusion is an example of what kind of irony?

   _____

4. On his last day of work before retirement, a policeman survives a fight with a burglar, a car chase with a speeder, and a shoot-out with a kidnapper, only to be struck dead by lightning as he walks home from work on a clear night. What is ironic about this scene?

   _____

Using Irony

On another sheet of paper, write the following scenarios:

1. A brief scenario of your own demonstrating verbal irony.
2. A brief scenario of your own demonstrating situational irony.
3. A brief scenario of your own demonstrating dramatic irony.

Reading Tip

When you read works of fiction, look for clues to ironic endings and occurrences. Sometimes hints occur and sometimes they do not. Is irony most effective when it's hinted at or when it's not?

Local Color

Definition

Local color: Writing that brings to life a specific region of a country. Dialect, customs, clothes, mannerisms, landscape descriptions, and character types and attitudes all help to create local color.

Examples from Literature

Willa Cather brings to life Nebraska in the early 1900s through descriptions of both customs and scenery in *My Antonia.*

> *Customs:* Before we went to bed, Jake and Otto were called up to the living-room for prayers. Grandfather put on silver-rimmed spectacles and read several Psalms.

> *Scenery:* Our neighbors lived in sod houses and dugouts—comfortable, but not very roomy. Our white frame house, with a storey and a half-storey above the basement, stood at the east end of what I might call the farmyard with the windmill close by the kitchen door.

Sherwood Anderson brings to life the fields of Ohio in autumn in this description from "Sophistication":

> On the Trunion Pike, where the road after it left town stretched away between berry fields now covered with dry brown leaves, the dust from passing wagons arose in clouds. Children, curled into little balls, slept on the straw scattered on wagon beds. Their hair was full of dust and their fingers black and sticky. The dust rolled away over the fields and the departing sun set it ablaze with colors.

Locating Local Color

Sarah Orne Jewett, Mary Wilkins Freeman, and Harriet Beecher Stowe all wrote about New England following the Civil War. For each passage below, decide which technique(s) the author has used to give the reader the flavor of New England in the late 1800s. Indicate your responses in the spaces provided.

Local Color Techniques

a. dialect
b. scenery
c. clothing
d. mannerisms
e. customs
f. attitudes

_____ 1. "Well, dear," she said sorrowfully, "I've took great advantage o' your bein' here. I ain't had such a season for years, but I have never had nobody I could so trust."
　　　　　—Sarah Orne Jewett, "The Country of the Pointed Firs"

_____ 2. Louisa tied a green apron round her waist, and got out a flat straw hat with a green ribbon. Then she went into the garden with a little blue crockery bowl, to pick some currants for her tea.
　　　　　—Mary Wilkins Freeman,
　　　　　A New England Nun and Other Stories

_____ 3. The site of Brunswick is a sandy plain on which the college buildings seem to have been dropped for the good old Yankee economic reason of using land for public buildings that could not be used for anything else…. But these sandy plains, these pine forests, were neighbors to the great, lively, musical blue ocean whose life-giving presence made itself seen, heard, and felt every hour of the day and night.
　　　　　—Harriet Beecher Stowe, "A Student's Sea Story"

Creating Local Color

On another sheet of paper, use descriptions of dialect, scenery, clothing, mannerisms, customs, and attitudes to help you paint the picture of the following regions in one or two descriptive paragraphs.

1. A Texas ranch
2. Hollywood
3. Las Vegas
4. New York City
5. The Rocky Mountains

Reading Tip

Read a short story that brings to life a specific locale. Then try to draw or paint the region you have read about. Here are some reading options: Bret Harte writes tales set in California mining camps; Sherwood Anderson writes stories set in early 1900s Ohio; Mark Twain writes of the Mississippi riverfront.

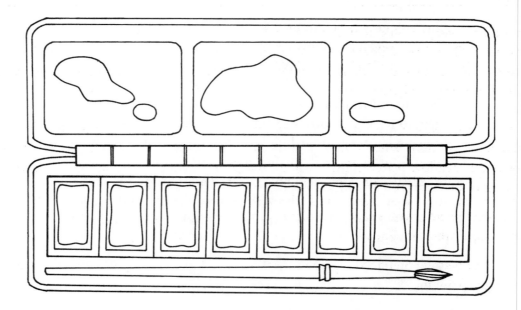

Mood and Tone

Definitions

Mood: The feeling created in a reader by a literary work. Setting, description, events, and tone all contribute to a story's atmosphere or mood. A story's mood may be joyous or sorrowful, hopeful or discouraged, for example.

Tone: The attitude an author takes toward his subject, character, or reader. Tone is created through word choice and details. A story's tone may be serious or humorous, angry or sympathetic, for example. A reader can miss the entire point of a story if the author's tone is misunderstood.

Examples from Literature

The mood of Chief Joseph's "I Will Fight No More Forever" speech is one of sorrow and hopelessness: "The little children are freezing to death. My people, some of them, have run away to the hills and have no blankets, no food.… Hear me, my chiefs, I am tired; my heart is sick and sad. From where the sun now stands, I will fight no more forever."

Anton Chekhov's play *A Marriage Proposal* is an account of Lomov's proposal to his neighbor's daughter, Natalia. When Lomov's proposal attempt turns into a petty argument about who owns the meadow between their homes, the author's comic approach to presenting the argument sets a tone of fun and mockery:

NATALIA: And if you keep on explaining it for two days, and put on five suits of evening clothes, the meadows are still ours, ours, ours!

LOMOV: Natalia Stepanova, I don't need the meadows.… I beg of you, accept them as a gift from me!

NATALIA: But I can give them to you, because they belong to me.

Recognizing Mood and Tone

The tone of Mark Twain's novel *Adventures of Huckleberry Finn* alternates between serious and humorous depending on the scene. Decide which passages below are meant to make you laugh and which are intended to be taken seriously. Write "serious" or "humorous" in the spaces provided.

_____ 1. My nose begun to itch. It itched till the tears come into my eyes. But I dasn't scratch. Then it begun to itch on the inside. Next I got to itching underneath. I didn't know how I was going to set still.... I was itching in eleven different places now.

_____ 2. I says to myself, they'll follow the track of that sackful of rocks to the shore and then drag the river for me. And they'll follow that meal track to the lake and go browsing down the creek that leads out of it to find the robbers that killed me and took the things. They won't even hunt the river for anything but my dead carcass. They'll soon get tired of that, and won't bother no more about me.

_____ 3. Then Miss Watson she took me in the closet and prayed, but nothing come of it. She told me to pray every day, and whatever I asked for I would get it. But it warn't so. I tried it. Once I got a fish-line, but no hooks. It warn't any good to me without hooks. I tried for the hooks three or four times, but somehow I couldn't make it work.

_____ 4. When I lit my candle and went up to my room that night there sat pap—his own self!... I had shut the door too. Then I turned around, and there he was. I used to be scared of him all the time, he tanned me so much. I reckoned I was scared now, too; but in a minute I see I was mistaken—that is, after the first jolt, as you may say, when my breath sort of hitched, he being so unexpected; but right away after I see I warn't scared of him worth bothering about.

Matching Tones and Moods

Match each tone or mood with the passage that illustrates it.

Moods

a. hopeless
b. gloomy
c. lighthearted
d. remorseful
e. fearful

_____ 1. When the banker had read this, he laid the paper on the table, kissed the strange man on the head, and went out of the lodge weeping. At no other time, even when he had lost heavily on the Stock Exchange, had he felt so great a contempt for himself. When he got home he lay on his bed, but his tears and emotion kept him for hours from sleeping.
　　　　　—Anton Chekhov, "The Bet"

_____ 2. Deep into the darkness peering, long I stood there wondering, fearing / Doubting, dreaming dreams no mortals ever dared to dream before.
　　　　　—Edgar Allan Poe, "The Raven"

_____ 3. We rubber plants form the connecting link between the vegetable kingdom and the decorations of a Waldorf-Astoria scene in a Third Avenue theater. I haven't looked up our family tree, but I believe we were raised by grafting a gum overshoe on to a 30-cent table d'hote stalk of asparagus.
　　　　　—O. Henry, "The Rubber Plant's Story"

_____ 4. At length, I found myself, as the shades of the evening drew on, within view of the melancholy House of Usher. I know not how it was—but, with the first glimpse of the building, a sense of insufferable gloom pervaded my spirit.
　　　　　—Edgar Allan Poe, "The Fall of the House of Usher"

_____ 5. One dollar and eighty-seven cents.... And the next day would be Christmas. There was clearly nothing to do but flop down on the shabby little couch and howl. So Della did it. Which instigates the moral reflection that life is made up of sobs, sniffles, and smiles, with sniffles predominating.
　　　　　—O. Henry, "The Gift of the Magi"

Moral and Theme

Definitions

Moral: The lesson expressed in a simple story. Fables and parables are specifically designed to teach a moral, which often appears in a single statement at the end. In more complex stories, lessons and other messages about human nature are buried in the text.

Theme: Indirectly expressed insights. Most literary works have at least one theme. Many express several themes that are tied together.

Examples from Literature

Aesop's fables state clear-cut morals such as this one from "The Wolf in Sheep's Clothing": "Appearances are often deceiving."

O. Henry's "The Gift of the Magi" expresses a theme of selfless love that is stated almost as a simple moral at the end of the story. After hearing about a man and woman who give away their own prized possessions to purchase treasures for each other, the reader is clued in to the story's theme/moral: "But in a last word to the wise of these days let it be said that of all who give gifts these two were the wisest. Of all who give and receive gifts, such as they are wisest. Everywhere they are wisest. They are the Magi."

Themes in Louisa May Alcott's *Little Women* include the independence of the human spirit and the positive ties of family.

Concluding a Moral

The last line of this Aesop's fable states its moral. See if you can fill in the last line after reading the fable.

The Ant and the Grasshopper

In a field one summer's day a Grasshopper was hopping about, chirping and singing to its heart's content. An Ant passed by, bearing along with great toil an ear of corn he was taking to the nest.

"Why not come and chat with me," said the Grasshopper, "instead of toiling and moiling in that way?"

"I am helping to lay up food for the winter," said the Ant, "and recommend you do the same."

"Why bother about winter?" said the Grasshopper; we have got plenty of food at present." But the Ant went on its way and continued its toil. When the winter came the Grasshopper had no food and found itself dying of hunger, while it saw the ants distributing every day corn and grain from the stores they had collected in the summer.

Then the Grasshopper knew: _____

_____ .

The Dove and the Ant

An Ant, going to a river to drink, fell in, and was carried along in the stream. A Dove pitied her condition, and threw into the river a small bough, by means of which the Ant gained the shore. The Ant, afterward, seeing a man with a fowling-piece aiming at the Dove, stung him in the foot sharply, and made him miss his aim, and so saved the Dove's life.

What might be the moral of this fable?

_____

_____

_____

Writing Morals

Choose one of the morals below and, on a separate sheet of paper, write a fable of your own that expresses this moral. Use animal characters and a short and simple story to make your point.

> The early bird gets the worm.
> Love conquers all.
> Treat others as you wish to be treated.
> Leave well enough alone.
> Practice makes perfect.
> Be yourself.

Recognizing Theme

List one or more of the themes of these well-known stories or screenplays.

1. *Beauty and the Beast* _____

2. *Babe* _____

3. *Charlotte's Web* _____

4. *Pinocchio* _____

5. *Monsters, Inc.* _____

Writing Exercise

Try to develop one of the morals listed above into the central theme of a well-developed short story.

Reading Exercise

Look for multiple themes in complex novels and short stories. How do authors tie themes together? How do multiple themes fit into a single plot?

Narrator/Point of View

Definitions

Narrator: The voice telling a story. Narration keeps a story moving, filling in details and description between dialogue. The narrator speaks from one of several points of view.

Point of view: The narrator's position with respect to the characters and the reader. Point of view helps determine what a reader is told and when, and how a reader feels about characters and events in a story. There are different types of points of view:

First person: One of the story's characters narrates using the pronoun *I*.

Second person: This point of view places the reader in a story using the pronoun *you*.

Limited third person: The narrator is outside of the story, and sees events through the eyes of only one character. Limited third person uses the pronouns *she* and *he*.

All-knowing third person: The narrator is not one of the characters in the story, but rather narrates as though looking in on the story and seeing the emotions, motives, and actions of all the characters. The narrator uses the pronouns *he* and *she*.

Examples from Literature

Edgar Allan Poe's "A Predicament" is narrated from the first person point of view: "It was a quiet and still afternoon when I strolled forth in the goodly city of Edina...."

The all-knowing, third-person narrator in Louisa May Alcott's *An Old Fashioned Girl* sees both the actions of Fanny and her brother: "'If I was president I'd make a law to shut up all boys till they were grown...' said Fanny, as she watched...her brother strolling down the street. She might have changed her mind, however, if she had followed him, for as soon as he turned the corner, his whole aspect altered."

Identifying Points of View

Decide whether each of the following passages is written in first, second, or third person. Indicate your responses in the spaces provided.

1. If your head is wax; don't walk in the sun.
      —Benjamin Franklin, *Poor Richard's Almanack*

   Person: _____

2. About the year 1727, just at the time that earthquakes were prevalent in New England, and shook many tall sinners down upon their knees, there lived near this place a meager, miserly fellow of the name of Tom Walker.
      —Washington Irving, "The Devil and Tom Walker"

   Person: _____

3. When he placed his guest in front of the dying man, Hard-Heart, after a pause, that proceeded as much from sorrow as decorum, leaned a little forward and demanded, "Does my father hear the words of his son?"
      —James Fenimore Cooper, *The Prairie*

   Person: _____

4. A slip of the foot you may soon recover, but a slip of the tongue you may never get over.
      —Benjamin Franklin, *Poor Richard's Almanack*

   Person: _____

5. It was a mystery all insolvable; nor could I grapple with the shadowy fancies that crowded upon me as I pondered.
      —Edgar Allan Poe, "The Fall of the House of Usher"

   Person: _____

6. It was quite late in the evening when the little Moss came snugly to anchor, and Queegueg and I went ashore; so we could attend to no business that day, at least none but a supper and bed.
      —Herman Melville, *Moby Dick*

   Person: _____

Using Narration

Practice using narration techniques by completing the following exercises in the spaces provided.

1. Relate the scene of an argument using no dialogue.

   _____

   _____

   _____

   _____

2. Describe your bedroom. In your description, relate the sights, sounds, smells, tastes, and textures.

   _____

   _____

   _____

   _____

3. Tell about your favorite movie using no dialogue.

   _____

   _____

   _____

   _____

Using Point of View

On a separate piece of paper, use both dialogue and description to create a scene wherein a student has an awful day at school. Write the scene in each point of view: first person, second person, limited third person, and all-knowing third person.

Reading Exercise

Identify the point of view used in stories you read. How does point of view affect your feelings about characters and events in a story?

32 Plot

Definition

Plot: The sequence of events that make up a story. The plot serves as a skeleton on which the other elements of a story (characters, setting, etc.) hang. A plot usually involves the unfolding and solving of a conflict. Plots can be simple or complex. Most novels include a main plot and one or more subplots. A common plot structure consists of the following parts:

Exposition: An introduction to the characters and setting of a story.

Rising action: The development of complications that create the conflict of a story.

Climax or *turning point:* The crisis to which the rising action has been leading. The climax is the point of highest tension in a story. It serves as the turning point between the rising and falling action.

Falling action: Events that lead to a conflict's resolution. Characters learn to deal with life after the crisis in the falling action.

Resolution: The point at which the conflict is resolved and the story is brought to a natural or surprising end.

Example from Literature

Frank Stockton's "The Lady, or the Tiger?" follows the standard plot line with one exception: it leaves the resolution open to reader opinion. The story begins with an exposition: "In the very olden time, there lived a semibarbaric king." The rising action unfolds a situation in which the boyfriend of the king's daughter is in trouble with the law. The climax occurs when the boyfriend must choose between the door to a room containing a tiger who will eat him and one containing a woman whom he will have to marry. The falling action discusses the philosophy behind his decision, and the resolution is left to the reader: "Which came out of the opened door—the lady, or the tiger?"

Identifying Parts of a Plot

"The Most Dangerous Game" by Richard Connell is the story of a man who hunts other men. The story line appears below, but has been written out of order. Put the story in order by numbering the events from 1 to 5 and identifying each part: (1) exposition, (2) rising action, (3) climax, (4) falling action, or (5) resolution.

_____ _____ Rainsford is up in a tree. The dogs are close on his trail. General Zaroff is right behind them. Zaroff's giant assistant is beside him. Rainsford must decide now what he will do. He plunges into the sea.

_____ _____ A mysterious island in the middle of the sea is described to the reader. The reader is introduced to Rainsford, a man shipwrecked on the island, and General Zaroff, the island's owner and sole resident, with the exception of his large and brutish servant, Ivan.

_____ _____ Rainsford and General Zaroff discuss hunting at dinner. General Zaroff hints that he is bored of hunting animals and has begun to hunt humans. Rainsford is to be his next prey.

_____ _____ Zaroff goes off to bed. When he arrives in his room, "A man who had been hiding in the curtains of the bed, was standing there." The general is shocked to see that Rainsford is still alive, but thrilled that the adventure continues. "On guard, Rainsford," he says. And in the end, the reader is informed, "He had never slept in a better bed, Rainsford decided."

_____ _____ Zaroff, assuming Rainsford has drowned, returns home and makes himself a nice dinner.

Developing a Plot

Use the format below to develop the outline of a plot for a story about a basketball team. You do not need to use complete sentences in your outline. Just indicate in general what will happen during each phase of the story's plot. The climax of the story has been provided.

Exposition:

_____

_____

_____

Rising action:

_____

_____

_____

Climax:

It's the championship game. The score is 45 to 46. There are 20 seconds left. The protagonist is fouled. He takes his shot.

Falling action:

_____

_____

_____

Resolution:

_____

_____

_____

Poetic License

Definition

Poetic license: An author's right to break the rules of proper writing in order to achieve an effect or get a point across. Poetry often disregards punctuation rules to preserve both a visual and rhythmic effect. Speeches sometimes contain incomplete sentences in favor of strong phrases that achieve parallelism and power. Fiction and nonfiction writers both invent words and phrases to fit new and unique ideas, inventions, and situations. Advertisers often disregard spelling, punctuation, and capitalization rules to add emphasis, express uniqueness, or create a mood.

Examples from Literature

Abraham Lincoln began sentences with the words "but" and "and" for the sake of emphasis in his debates with Douglas: "And I will remind Judge Douglas and his audience…. But if the judge continues to put forward the declaration that…."

Shakespeare coined many new phrases to suit his needs. The idea of waiting with "bated breath," for example, first appeared in his 1596 play *The Merchant of Venice.*

In his introduction to *A Christmas Carol,* Charles Dickens capitalizes words mid-sentence for emphasis: "I have endeavored in this Ghostly little book, to raise the Ghost of an Idea…."

At the end of the poem "Mannahatta," Walt Whitman uses incomplete sentences to maintain the piece's rhythm and mood:

> City of hurried and sparkling waters! city of spires and masts!
> City nested in bays! my city!

Locating Poetic License Usage

Find examples of authors' use of poetic license in your literature textbook, library books, or advertisements in magazines or on product packaging. Record the samples you find under the appropriate headings below, and give the source for each.

Improper use of capitalization

1. _____

2. _____

Subject-verb agreement errors

1. _____

2. _____

Run-on sentences

1. _____

2. _____

Improper use of punctuation

1. _____

2. _____

Spelling errors

1. _____

2. _____

License to Create

Poetic license allows authors to make up words and ignore language conventions in order to be creative. Use your license to create in the following exercises.

A. Coin your own terms for the following situations:

    1. A car swerving around a curve might be said to _____

    2. A three-legged dog might be called a _____

    3. The sound a trumpet makes in its highest register: _____

    4. The feeling of getting into a warm bed on a cold night: _____

    5. The taste of sour pickles: _____

B. Write a poem about peace using only lower-case letters to give it a feel of quietness.

C. Create a sense of hurriedness by writing a run-on sentence about a busy day.

D. Use incomplete sentences for emphasis in a paragraph about freedom.

Reading Tip

The author e.e. cummings was famous for his disregard for language conventions. Read some of his poetry at your school's library or on the Internet.

34 **Pun**

Definition

Pun: A play on words. Some puns rely on different meanings connected to the same word. Some puns rely on different words sounding similar. Most puns are humorous, although some are serious.

Examples from Literature

A pun relying on different meanings connected to the same word

In Norton Juster's *The Phantom Tollbooth*, Milo, the book's main character, finds himself in a land called Dictionopolis where words are often taken both literally and figuratively at the same time. This causes some confusion for Milo when he orders a *light* meal:

> The waiters rushed in carrying large serving platters and set them on the table in front of the king. When he lifted the covers, shafts of brilliant-colored light leaped from the plates and bounced around the ceiling, the walls, across the floor, and out the window.

A pun relying on two words sounding similar

Later, when another character offers Milo a dessert option, the pun is funny because the word *synonym* sounds similar to the word *cinnamon*: " 'Perhaps you'd care for a synonym bun,' suggested the duke."

The John Donne poem "Hymn to God the Father" makes a serious comparison of the son of God to the sun in the sky: "But swear by Thy self, that at my death Thy Son Shall shine as he shines now...."

Shakespeare makes extensive use of puns in his plays, including this one spoken by a dying character in *Romeo and Juliet*: "Ask for me tomorrow and you shall find me a *grave* man."

Understanding Puns

On a separate sheet of paper, answer the following questions.

1. Why is the pun about light in *A Phantom Tollbooth* funny?
   When Milo changes his order from a light meal to a square meal, what do you think he is served?
2. Why do you think puns are humorous?
3. How do you think puns first came into use?

Punny Jokes

A. Decide which puns here rely on similar sounding words and which rely on different meanings of the same word. Record your responses in the spaces provided.

1. I hoped one of the ten puns I entered in a contest would win, but no pun in ten did.

   _____

2. When a ship carrying blue paint ran into a ship carrying red paint, both ships were sunk and the crew members of each were *marooned* on a nearby island.

   _____

3. Two boll weevil brothers went out into the world. One made it big in Hollywood and the other simply became the lesser of two weevils.

   _____

B. See if you can solve these cow riddles that rely on puns.

1. What do you get when you milk a pampered cow?

   _____

2. What do you get when you milk a brown cow?

   _____

3. What do you get when you shake a cow before milking her?

   _____

4. What do you get when you feed a cow toast before milking her?

   _____

Writing Puns

A. Using your knowledge of puns, match the fictitious book titles below with their supposed authors.

_____	1. *Babe, the Autobiography*	a.	Rock N. Roll
_____	2. *Carpooling Today*	b.	Miss Debuss
_____	3. *Do-It-Yourself Auto Repairs*	c.	Sam Witch
_____	4. *Be Prepared*	d.	Ivor Gott
_____	5. *Basic Dog Training*	e.	Ima Pig
_____	6. *Walk to Work*	f.	Axel Grease
_____	7. *Lunch on the Run*	g.	Jose Cannusee
_____	8. *Basic Memory Skills*	h.	Kay Nine
_____	9. *The History of the Star Spangled Banner*	i.	Justin Case
_____	10. *The Story of Elvis*	j.	Cher A. Ride

B. Now invent some of your own book titles and authors that make use of puns.

1. _____

2. _____

3. _____

4. _____

5. _____

Reading Tip

Enter a wonderful world of puns by reading *The Phantom Tollbooth* or *Alice in Wonderland* in their entirety.

Rhetorical Question

Definition

Rhetorical question: A question that does not require an answer. Usually, the answer to a rhetorical question is, in fact, obvious. The rhetorical question is used in persuasive writing to emphasize and bolster an argument.

Examples from Literature

Sojourner Truth's famous Akron, Ohio, speech given at a women's rights convention in 1851 uses a rhetorical question to remind listeners that black females are women too:

> Nobody ever helps me into carriages, or over mud-puddles, or gives me any best place! And ain't I a woman? Look at me! Look at my arm! I have ploughed and planted, and gathered into barns, and no man could head me! And ain't I a woman? I could work as much and eat as much as a man—when I could get it—and bear the lash as well! And ain't I a woman? I have borned thirteen children, and seen them all sold off to slavery, and when I cried out with my mother's grief, none but Jesus heard me! And ain't I a woman?

In his second round of debates with Douglas, Abraham Lincoln uses rhetorical questions to emphasize that the truth is the truth whether popular or not: "Is it the true test of a soundness of a doctrine, that in some places people won't let you hear it? Is that the way to test the truth of any doctrine?"

Interpreting Rhetorical Questions

Patrick Henry gave a famous speech at the Virginia Convention in which he tried to convince colonists of the necessity of rebellion against the British. Read each of the following rhetorical questions from that speech. Then decide what point he is trying to make by asking each question. Indicate your responses on the lines provided.

1. Question: "And judging by the past, I wish to know what there has been in the conduct of the British ministry for the last ten years to justify those hopes [for equality] with which gentleman have been pleased to solace themselves and the house?"

   Point: _____

2. Question: "And what have we to oppose them? Shall we try argument? Sir, we have been trying that for the last ten years. Have we anything new to offer on the subject?"

   Point: _____

3. Question: "Shall we resort to entreaty and humble supplication? What terms shall we find which have not been already exhausted?"

   Point: _____

4. Question: "They tell us, sir, that we are weak—unable to cope with so formidable an adversary. But when shall we be stronger? Will it be the next week, or the next year? Will it be when a British guard shall be stationed in every house? Shall we gather strength by irresolution and inaction?"

   Point: _____

5. Question: "Why stand we here idle? What is it that gentlemen wish? What would they have? Is life so dear, or peace so sweet, as to be purchased at the price of chains and slavery?"

   Point: _____

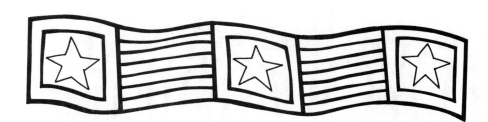

Using Rhetorical Questions

Prove the following points through the use of rhetorical questions. A sample has been completed for you.

> Point: People are good by nature.
> Question: Does not every one of us start life as a beautiful innocent infant?

1. Point: Literature opens up the world to its readers.

   Question: _____

2. Point: To succeed in life, you need to graduate from high school.

   Question: _____

3. Point: The United States is a melting pot.

   Question: _____

4. Point: Music is the universal language.

   Question: _____

5. Point: Necessity is the mother of invention.

   Question: _____

6. Point: Two heads are better than one.

   Question: _____

7. Point: Sometimes it pays to procrastinate.

   Question: _____

8. Point: Sometimes cheaper isn't better.

   Question: _____

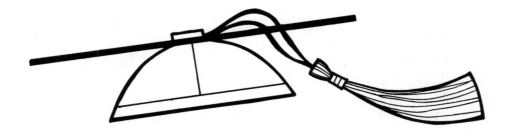

Satire, Parody, and Farce

Definitions

Satire: Writing that makes fun of habits, ideas, or weaknesses in a person, an institution, an entire society, or humanity in general. Satire can be witty and tolerant or biting and vicious. It is often written with the intent of exposing or correcting a problem.

Parody: Writing that makes fun of a piece (or entire genre) of literature, art, or music. Parodies imitate tone, mood, language, theme, and/or form, sometimes by using exaggeration.

Farce: Writing that features slapstick, far-fetched, and ridiculous humor that may include physical comedy, practical jokes, exaggeration, and absurdity.

Examples from Literature

Ezra Pound satirizes abstract art in "L'Art":

> Green arsenic smeared on an egg-white cloth,
> Crushed strawberries! Come, let us feast our eyes.

Jane Austen's *Northanger Abbey* is a parody of Gothic romance novels wherein a young heroine must meet up with a hero and live happily ever after:

> There was not one family among their acquaintance who had reared and supported a boy accidentally found at their door.... But when a young lady is to be a heroine.... Something must and will happen to throw a hero in her way.

Petty arguments and health problems stand in the way of Lomov asking Natalia to marry him in the Anton Chekhov farce *A Marriage Proposal*:

> LOMOV: If you will be so good as to remember, my meadows touch your birchwoods.
> NATALIA: Pardon the interruption. You said "my meadows"—but are they yours?
> LOMOV: Yes, they belong to me.
> NATALIA: What nonsense! the meadows belong to us—not to you!

Categorizing Satires, Parodies, and Farces

In the space provided, identify each of the following descriptions and passages as satire, parody, or farce.

1. Silly word play dialogue in Shakespeare's *Twelfth Night* develops into an entire scene of absurd conversation, which begins:

   CLOWN: No, sir, I live by the church.
   VIOLA: Art thou a churchman?
   CLOWN: No such matter, sir: I do live by the church; for I do live at my house, and my house doth stand by the church.
   VIOLA: So, thou mayst say, the king lies by a beggar, if a beggar dwell near him.

   _____

2. The movie *Space Balls* is a spoof of the movie *Star Wars*.

   _____

3. Weird Al's song *Jurassic Park* makes fun of both the song "Someone Left the Cake Out in the Rain" and the movie *Jurassic Park*.

   _____

4. In Jonathan Swift's *Gulliver's Travels*, the author compares the petty arguments between the Catholics and the Protestants to a debate about which end of a boiled egg to crack first:

   The primitive way of breaking eggs, before we eat them, was upon the larger end; but his present majesty's grandfather, while he was a boy, going to eat an egg, and breaking it according to the ancient practice, happened to cut one of his fingers. Whereupon the emperor his father published an edict, commanding all his subjects, upon great penalties, to break the small end of their eggs. The people so highly resented this law, that our histories tell us there have been six rebellions raised on that account;...

   _____

5. The haughty character of Hepzibah Pyncheon in Nathaniel Hawthorne's *The House of Seven Gables* makes fun of the pride of upper-class people.

   _____

Writing Satires, Parodies, and Farces

1. In a paragraph, satirize a glamorous movie star on a camping trip.

   _____

   _____

   _____

   _____

2. Write a parody of an action movie theme song to the tune of *Twinkle, Twinkle, Little Star*.

   _____

   _____

   _____

3. Outline the plot of a farce based on the absurd situation of an alien clown landing on earth. Be certain to include physical comedy, jokes, exaggeration, and absurdity.

   Exposition: _____

   _____

   Rising action: _____

   _____

   Climax: _____

   _____

   Falling action: _____

   _____

   Resolution: _____

   _____

Viewing Tip

Rent and enjoy one of the many black-and-white farce films featuring Laurel and Hardy or The Three Stooges.

Story Within a Story

Definition

Story within a story: A plot technique in which an inner story is set inside the framework of another story. As opposed to a flashback, an inner story is not simply past events reported to provide insight into current characters or events, but rather is a fully developed tale that takes over and becomes the main story.

Examples from Literature

In Saki's "The Storyteller," two stories are told within the framework of a tale about a woman trying to entertain children on a train by telling them a parable. When the parable does not excite the children, a stranger sitting in the same car begins a tale that becomes the basis of a story within a story:

> "Once upon a time," began the bachelor, "there was a little girl called Bertha, who was extraordinarily good."

In "The Celebrated Jumping Frog of Calaveras County," Mark Twain sets the tale of a gambling man and his jumping frog inside the framework of another story:

> Simon Wheeler backed me into a corner and blockaded me there with his chair, and then sat down and reeled off the monotonous narrative which follows this paragraph.

The story that follows, "There was a feller here once by the name of Jim Smiley....", is anything but monotonous and carries the reader along so splendidly, he or she forgets there even is a framework story.

Locating a Story Within a Story

The following excerpt is taken from Mark Twain's tale "A Story Without an End." Underline the sentence in which the inner story takes over.

We had one game in the ship which was a good time passer—at least it was at night in the smoking room when the men were getting freshened up from the day's monotonies and dullnesses. It was the completion of noncomplete stories. That is to say, a man would tell off a story except the finish, then the others would try to supply the ending out of their own invention.... But the story which called out the most persistent and determined and ambitious effort was one which *had* no ending, and so there was nothing to compare the new-made endings with.... [The man who told it] would give anyone fifty dollars who would finish the story to the satisfaction of a jury to be appointed by ourselves.... In substance the storiette was as follows:

John Brown, aged thirty-one, good, gentle, bashful, timid, lived in a quiet village in Missouri.... Mary Taylor, twenty-three, modest, sweet, winning, and in character and person beautiful, was all in all to him, and he was very near all in all to her. She was wavering, but his hopes were high.... At last the time was ripe for a final advance.... He took to the road.... When he was four miles out on the lonely road and was walking his horse over a wooden bridge, his straw hat blew off and fell in the creek.... He must have that hat...but how was he to get it? Then he had an idea.... Yes he would risk it.... He undressed and put his clothes in the buggy...then hurried to the stream. He swam out and soon had the hat. When he got to the top of the bank the horse was gone!

Interpreting a Story Within a Story

1. Who are the main characters of the framework story in "A Story Without an End"?

   _____

2. What is the main conflict in the framework story in "A Story Without an End"?

   _____

3. Who are likely to be two of the main characters in the inner story in "A Story Without an End"?

   _____

4. The inner story in "A Story Without an End" continues with John Brown chasing his horse, hopping into his buggy, and throwing on his shirt, tie, and coat. As he reaches for his pants, he meets women along the road so he quickly throws a lap robe over his legs thinking he can finish dressing as soon as he passes by the women. (Lap robes were blankets placed over one's legs while riding in a buggy on cool days.) Unfortunately, the women stop John and several humorous things happen that prevent him from being able to get his pants on. One of the women, of course, is Mary Taylor, and another of them is Mary's mother, who does not have a fondness for John. Knowing these details, why might the inner story take over the framework story in "A Story Without an End"? Write your answer on a separate sheet of paper.

5. Mark Twain returns his readers to the framework story just as Mary is about to share a buggy ride (and lap robe) with John, who has, up to this point, been too shy to explain his predicament. Back on the ship of the framework story, there is not a single sailor who can end the tale satisfactorily in keeping with John's gentle and bashful nature. How would you end the inner story? Write your answer on a separate sheet of paper.

Writing Exercise

Try your hand at writing a story within a story. Make the framework story involve a main character who is camping with friends. Late at night, around a bonfire, he is asked to tell a ghost story, which becomes the tale's inner story.

Stream of Consciousness

Definition

Stream of consciousness: A narrative style in which thoughts, feelings, and emotions are recorded as they occur. The style gives the reader the impression that the author (or character) is thinking aloud. Sentence structure and punctuation rules may be ignored, and recorded thoughts and feelings may be disconnected in stream-of-consciousness writing.

Stream of consciousness appears in poetry, short stories, and novels. Narratives written in this style may lack chronological order. The story line may not come together until late in the reading when the reader can put together disconnected narrative.

Examples from Literature

James Joyce's *A Portrait of the Artist as a Young Man* records the thoughts, images, and emotions flowing through the mind of a child named Stephen:

> Once upon a time and a very good time it was there was a moocow coming down along the road and this moocow that was coming down along the road met a nicens little boy named baby tuckoo. His father told him the story: his father looked at him through a glass: he had a hairy face. He was baby tuckoo. The moocow came down the road where Betty Byrne lived: she sold lemon platt.

Ambrose Bierce begins "An Occurrence at Owl Creek Bridge" with a matter-of-fact account of events as they occur. His narrative has more regard for sentence structure and punctuation, but still flows freely from the narrator's mind:

> A man stood upon a railroad bridge in northern Alabama, looking down into the swift water twenty feet below. The man's hands were behind his back, the wrists bound with a cord.

Understanding Stream of Consciousness

1. James Joyce uses stream of consciousness to relate the story of a child in *A Portrait of the Artist as a Young Man*. Why is stream of consciousness especially effective in relating the thoughts of a child?

   _____

   _____

2. Stream-of-consciousness style creates an artistic piece rather than a formal-sounding literary work. Certain story lines, characters, themes, and moods especially benefit from the use of the style. Describe three writing situations that would benefit from the use of the stream-of-consciousness narrative style.

   _____

   _____

   _____

Explaining Stream of Consciousness

The following passages exemplify stream of consciousness. In your own words, explain why each meets the criteria for that narrative style.

1. And indeed there will be time
   To wonder, "Do I dare?" and, "Do I dare?"
   Time to turn back and descend the stair,
   With a bald spot in the middle of my hair—
   (They will say: "How his hair is growing thin!")
       —T.S. Eliot, "The Love Song of J. Alfred Prufrock"

   Why is this stream of consciousness?

   _____

   _____

2. His mother had a nicer smell than his father. She played on the piano the sailor's hornpipe for him to dance. He danced: Tralala lala Tralala traladdy....
       —James Joyce, *A Portrait of the Artist as a Young Man*

   Why is this stream of consciousness?

   _____

   _____

Identifying Stream of Consciousness

Most narratives tell stories chronologically. Authors describe characters, events, and settings systematically as a story unfolds. Stream-of-consciousness writings; however, imitate the natural flow of thoughts and impressions as they go through a person's mind. Four story passages appear below. Circle the number in front of the two passages that exemplify stream-of-consciousness writing.

1. There was no hope for him this time: It was the third stroke. Night after night I had passed the house (it was vacation time) and studied the lighted square of window: and night after night I had found it lighted in the same way, faintly and evenly.
   —James Joyce, *The Dubliners*

2. He had risen from his chair and was standing between the parted blinds gazing down into the dull neutral-tinted London street. Looking over his shoulder, I saw that on the pavement opposite there stood a large woman with a heavy fur boa round her neck...and a broad-brimmed hat which was tilted in a coquettish Duchess of Devonshire fashion over her ear.
   —Sir Arthur Conan Doyle, *The Adventures of Sherlock Holmes*

3. Two months after they weighed anchor and cleared from the port of Freetown a half dozen British war vessels were scouring the south Atlantic for trace of them or their little vessel....
   —Edgar Rice Burroughs, *Tarzan of the Apes*

4. The silence was becoming a factory hum. Louder, and louder, till his ears hurt. The vibrations! Like a cacophony of machines and road gangs and roaring stadiums, the throbbing noise of humanity brawling and crashing about on the planet.
   —Slee Kabbala, *Ride*

Reading Tip

Look for samples of stream-of-consciousness style when you read.

39 Surprise Ending

Definition

Surprise ending: A conclusion to a narrative that is not expected by the reader. Surprise endings are most often foreshadowed throughout a story. A second reading of the tale reveals the subtle hints. Surprise endings are often abrupt, emotional, and ironic. They are frequently used to add poignancy to a point the author is trying to make.

Examples from Literature

Both the main character and the reader in Guy de Maupassant's "The Necklace" are surprised in the end to discover that a presumably expensive necklace, which has been borrowed and lost, was merely an imitation.

O. Henry was a master of the surprise ending. In his most famous tale, "The Gift of the Magi," he leads the reader through the agonizing choices of a young wife who cuts her prized hair to raise money to buy her husband a chain for his heirloom pocket watch. It is not until the end of the story that the reader learns of the husband's equally emotional day: He sold his treasured watch to buy his young wife fancy barrettes for her long, flowing hair.

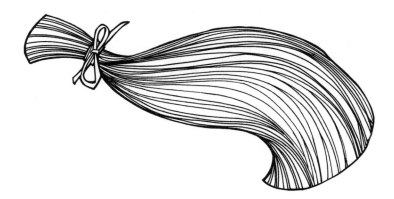

Predicting Surprise Endings

Read the following summaries of classic surprise-ending tales. Then predict their endings in the spaces provided.

1. In "Hearts and Hands" by O. Henry, Miss Fairchild boards a train and strikes up a conversation with an old acquaintance whom she finds to be handcuffed to another man. Mr. Easton, the old friend, tells Miss Fairchild all about his job as a sheriff. Then he and his handcuffed partner wander into another car. When the narrator focuses on the passengers in a seat nearby discussing the previous scene, the reader learns something that Miss Fairchild will never know.

   What might the reader learn at the end of this tale?

   _____

   _____

   _____

2. In Ambrose Bierce's "An Inhabitant of Carcosa," a man battling mental and physical illness wanders through a graveyard pondering what happens to spirits after they die. In the end, the man bends over to read the inscription on an ancient tombstone.

   What do you think the man learns?

   _____

   _____

   _____

3. In Jack Finney's *The Third Level,* Charlie speaks to his psychiatrist about his experience of locating a third level in Grand Central Station. On this level, the year is 1894. The psychiatrist, named Sam, suggests Charlie's time-travel experience was merely an illusion—an attempt to escape reality. Then Sam disappears. One day Charlie notices a stamp on an envelope in his stamp collection from the year 1894. He opens the envelope and reads the letter inside.

   Who is the letter from? What do you think it says?

   _____

   _____

   _____

Writing the Rest

Surprise endings often bring stories to a very abrupt close. The reader is left to imagine what might happen next based on the newly-discovered details. Because of the abruptness of surprise endings and the details they suddenly clarify about the story and the characters in general, surprise endings make great starting points for story sequels. Read the story summary below and then write a sequel on your own paper.

In Jack Finney's "The Face in the Photo," Inspector Martin O. Ihren questions Professor Weygand about a time travel machine he has been working on. The inspector is convinced that Professor Weygand has helped suspected criminals escape justice by transporting them to past times. In the end, Professor Weygand transports Inspector Ihren to the year 1893 against his will. What happens next? Does Ihren learn to like it in 1893? Does he find a way to get revenge on Weygand? Does he find a way to get back to the present? What happens next in the life of Weygand? Outline your sequel below and then write it on a separate piece of paper.

Exposition: _____

_____

Rising action: _____

_____

Climax: _____

_____

Falling action: _____

_____

Resolution: _____

_____

Viewing Tip

Look for surprise endings in movies. Think of the titles of some surprise-ending movies that spawned sequels.

Suspense

Definition

Suspense: A growing sense of tension or anxiety about what will happen next in a story. Suspense is usually most intense at the close of chapters in novels and the end of acts in dramas. "Tools" of suspense include mysterious circumstances such as locked doors and hidden rooms; mysterious characters such as monstrous creatures and peculiar-acting strangers; dark settings including thunderstorms and candle-lit rooms; difficult decisions such as whom to marry or whether to keep a secret; and unresolved issues such as whether or not a character will survive an illness or live through a perilous predicament such as hanging on the edge of a cliff.

Example from Literature

W.W. Jacob's "The Monkey's Paw" is full of suspense. The reader begins to wonder about the powers of the paw when its owner informs his audience, "It had a spell put on it by an old fakir." Although the spell gives the paw the power to grant wishes, the reader is still uncertain about its desirability. When the paw's owner is asked why he doesn't make a wish on the paw himself, his response is suspenseful:

"I have," he said, quietly, and his blotchy face whitened.

Questioning Suspense

Suspense raises a reader's anxiety level because it plants questions in his mind. In the following passages from Ambrose Bierce's "Moxon's Master," suspenseful details are in italics and preceded by a letter. What question does each italicized segment raise for the reader? Write your responses after each letter.

1. Moxon was (a) *speaking with unusual animation and earnestness.* As he paused I heard in an adjoining room known to me as his "machine-shop," which (b) *no one but himself was permitted to enter,* (c) *a singular thumping sound.*

   a. _____

   b. _____

   c. _____

2. Something forbade me either to enter or retire, (a) *a feeling—I know not how it came—that I was in the presence of imminent tragedy* and (b) *might serve my friend by remaining.*

   a. _____

   b. _____

Identifying Suspense Tools

Decide how each of the following phrases from "The Monkey's Paw" evokes suspense. In the spaces provided, choose from the following: (a) mysterious circumstances, (b) mysterious characters, (c) dark setting, (d) difficult decision, and (e) unresolved issue.

_____ 1. He sat alone in the darkness, gazing at the dying fire, and seeing faces in it.

_____ 2. The last face was so horrible and so simian that he gazed at it in amazement.

_____ 3. "I don't know what to wish for, and that's a fact," he said slowly.

_____ 4. As I wished, it twisted in my hand like a snake.

_____ 5. "Is anything the matter?" she asked breathlessly. "Has anything happened to Herbert? What is it? What is it?"

Locating Suspense

Review the tools of suspense defined on page 122. Then underline all the examples of suspense you find in this passage from Richard Connell's "The Most Dangerous Game."

"Do you think we've passed that island yet?"

"I can't tell in the dark. I hope so."

"Why?" asked Rainsford.

"The place has a reputation—a bad one."

"Cannibals?" suggested Rainsford.

"Hardly. Even cannibals wouldn't live in such a God-forsaken place. But it's gotten into sailor lore, somehow. Didn't you notice that the crew's nerves seemed a bit jumpy today?"

"They were a bit strange, now you mention it. Even Captain Nielsen—"

"Yes, even the tough-minded old Swede, who'd go up to the devil himself and ask him for a light. Those fishy blue eyes held a look I never saw there before. All I could get out of him was, 'This place has an evil name among seafaring men, sir.' Then he said to me, very gravely: 'Don't you feel anything?'—as if the air about us was actually poisonous. Now, you mustn't laugh when I tell you this—I did feel something like a sudden chill. There was no breeze. The sea was as flat as a plate-glass window. We were drawing near the island then. What I felt was a—a mental chill; a sort of sudden dread."

Reading Tip

Read a suspense novel and look for the suspense tools discussed in this book.

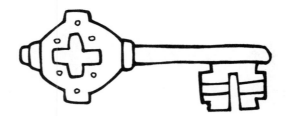

Review: Literary Terms and Techniques

Choose the best response to complete the following statements. Circle your answers.

1. A *stanza* would most often appear in
   a. a newspaper article
   b. a poem or song
   c. a novel
   d. a short story

2. In a poem, the reader is expected to pause at the end of
   a. an end-stopped line
   b. dialogue
   c. a run-on line
   d. an idiom

3. "I'm sitting on top of the world" is an example of
   a. symbolism
   b. personification
   c. an idiom
   d. parallelism

4. The *tone* of "Cinderella"
   a. never changes
   b. includes joy, sadness, and suspense
   c. is scary
   d. is angry

5. *The Phantom Tollbooth* is full of word plays called
   a. plots
   b. alliteration
   c. imagery
   d. puns

6. A *rhetorical question* might be used for all of the following reasons except
   a. to emphasize a point
   b. to provoke thought
   c. to gather information
   d. to improve a speech

7. The dictionary definition of a word is
   a. connotation
   b. symbolic definition
   c. image
   d. denotation

8. "I could eat a whole cow!" is an example of
   a. personification
   b. hyperbole
   c. conflict
   d. a surprise ending

9. An author famous for *surprise endings* is
   a. O. Henry
   b. Edgar Allan Poe
   c. Emily Dickinson
   d. Alice Walker

10. Weird Al songs that make fun of other songs are
    a. satires
    b. genres
    c. farces
    d. parodies

11. "Pretty pink pigs push pickles" is an example of
    a. dialect
    b. local color
    c. alliteration
    d. parallelism

12. Giving human qualities to something that is not human is called
    a. onomatopoeia
    b. assonance
    c. symbolism
    d. personification

13. Mark Twain stories contain all of the following except
    a. local color
    b. dialect
    c. characters
    d. refrains

14. All of the following are used to develop characters except
    a. physical descriptions
    b. character actions
    c. character speeches
    d. setting descriptions

15. A novel's storyline is called its
    a. plot
    b. moral
    c. theme
    d. conflict

16. *Conflict*
    a. often appears in poems
    b. can be internal or external
    c. is not part of most stories
    d. seldom drives character actions or decisions

17. The purposes of *foreshadowing* include all of the following except
    a. to create dramatic irony
    b. to create suspense
    c. to prepare the reader for a future event
    d. to tell the reader something that happened in the narrator's past

18. The three kinds of irony are (circle three)
    a. dramatic
    b. situational
    c. verbal
    d. external

19. An example of *onomatopoeia* is
    a. zip
    b. Ned needs a necktie
    c. fat cat
    d. The wind whistled his name.

20. "Kevin slept in longer than Rip Van Winkle" is an example of
    a. allusion
    b. alliteration
    c. genre
    d. flashback

Answer Key

Page 6: Understanding Denotation and Connotation

1. Spring denotes the season between winter and summer. It connotes youth, vitality, and energy. Autumn denotes the season between summer and winter. It connotes aging and loss of energy. Cold connotes aging, loss of vitality and health, and the recognition of pending death.

2. Dark denotes the absence of light. It connotes sorrow and depression.

3. To "be somebody" suggests social or material success. The phrase "I'm just a nobody" suggests the speaker does not believe himself to be socially important.

4. Answer will reflect student opinion, but might include laughter, family, and peace.

Page 6: Identifying Denotations and Connotations

1. d, g; 2. a, h; 3. c, i; 4. e, f; 5. b, j

Page 7: Recognizing Negative and Positive Connotations

Circle the following:
1. The Bargain Barn
2. Vintage Automobiles
3. The Ol' Fishin' Hole
4. Pasta Paradise
5. We carry only the highest quality footwear.
6. Clothes at a price you can afford.
7. Coziest cabin on the market today.
8. We employee highly skilled technicians.

Page 9: Identifying Hyperbole

Students should underline the phrases "they would almost have to lean up against a tree and take a rest," "in about one month I killed forty-seven more, which made one hundred and five bears I had killed in less than one year," "which shook the earth so, that we were rocked about like we had been in a cradle," and "swallow us up, like the big fish did Jonah."

Page 9: Understanding Hyperbole

Answers will reflect student opinion, but should demonstrate creative thought.

Page 10: Explaining Hyperbole

1. Student might suggest exaggeration adds excitement by allowing an author to write about unbelievable adventures. The absurdity of exaggerations makes them funny.

2. Student might suggest a politician should not make promises he can't keep if he is going to keep his constituents happy. Student might suggest hyperbole used in advertising will anger customers who do not get what they expect in a product.

3. Student answers will vary.

Page 10: Using Hyperbole

Student stories will vary.

Page 12: Defining Idioms

1. Sailors studied and discussed the tale.
2. Mary Taylor was important to him.
3. He strongly hoped for good results.
4. He would get the mother to agree with him.
5. Nobody was moving.
6. He began a journey.
7. They were all pleased and impressed.
8. Mrs. Enderby was best at planning.

Page 12: Illustrating Idioms

Student illustrations will vary. Drawings should reflect the idioms' intended meanings.

Page 12: Milo's Response

Student responses will vary.

Page 13: Using Idioms

Circle a fictional short story, a personal letter, a comic strip, movie dialogue, and a play.

Page 13: Stating Idioms

Student answers will vary.

Page 15: Interpreting Imagery

Student drawings will vary, but should include images from the poem passage.

Page 16: Using Imagery

Student answers will vary, but each paragraph should be descriptive enough for another student to identify the experience described.

Page 18: Locating Metaphors and Similes

1. The forest is compared to a church.

2. The earth is compared to a mother, and the sky is compared to a father.

3. Memories are compared to the links in a chain.

4. Winter is compared to the lid of a box. Cold winds blowing are compared to misery.

5. A rabbit's movements are compared to a flower, a gunshot, and a meteorite.

Page 19: Using Similes and Metaphors

Student similes and metaphors will vary. They should be identified as follows:

1. simile; 2. simile; 3. simile; 4. metaphor; 5. metaphor; 6. metaphor

Page 21: Defining Oxymorons

1. A working vacation is a vacation in which some work is completed along with the fun.

2. Acting normally is trying not to stand out or look suspicious.

3. A definite maybe indicates someone is undecided, but certainly considering the possibility of something.

4. Plastic glasses are eyeglasses made of plastic.

5. Found missing indicates someone or something has been discovered to be missing.

6. A small crowd indicates a medium-sized audience.

Page 21: Interpreting Paradoxes

1. Each failure helps us learn to succeed.

2. Gossip and lies are often more popular than the truth.

3. Being in a happy state at all times would take more energy than any of us has.

4. There is always more to learn.

5. Sometimes what is good for you is not pleasant.

6. Older people are wise, but haven't the energy to put their wisdom to good use, while young people have energy but little wisdom.

Page 22: Creating Oxymorons

A. 1. d; 2. b; 3. e; 4. a; 5. c

B. Student response will vary, but may approximate the following: 1. bright darkness; 2. truly insincere; 3. completely incomplete; 4. large miniature; 5. pretty ugly

Page 22: Creating Paradoxes

Student responses will vary, but should illustrate an understanding of paradoxes.

Page 24: Understanding and Identifying Personification

1. The animals boast, swagger, and pass away.

2. Life is personified.

3. The following words and phrases should be underlined: dreary road, gloomiest trees, stood aside, path creep

4. The following words and phrases should be underlined: so little has to do, butterflies to brood, bees to entertain, stir all day, Breezes fetch along, hold the sunshine in its lap, And bow.

Page 25: Interpreting Personification

1. a potato
2. "Let's go for a dip."
3. listen to their barks
4. because it was holding up the pants
5. the North and South poles
6. blubber gum

Page 25: Using Personification

Student responses will vary.

Page 27: Interpreting Symbols

1. The rose symbolizes love.

2. The rose symbolizes life and youth.

3. Answers will vary, but students should recognize the rose typically symbolizes positive things including youth, love, and beauty.

Page 28: Considering Common Symbols

1. j; 2. a; 3. h; 4. g; 5. c;
6. e; 7. i; 8. f; 9. d; 10. b

Page 28: Using Symbols

Student paragraphs will vary.

Page 30: Identifying Alliteration

Students should underline italicized portions:

1. Now *Beowulf bode in the burg* of the Scyldings,
   leader beloved, and long he ruled
   in *fame with all folk, since his father* had gone
   away from the world, till awoke an heir,
   haughty Healfdene, who held through life,
   sage and sturdy, the Scyldings glad.
   Then, *one after one, there woke* to him,
   to the *chieftain of clansmen, children* four.

2. Once upon a midnight dreary, while I pondered, *weak and weary*,...

   While I *nodded, nearly napping*, suddenly there came a tapping,...

   Doubting, dreaming dreams no mortal ever dared to dream before;...

   Open here I fling the shutter, when with many a *flirt and flutter*,...

   Nothing further then he uttered, not a *feather then he fluttered*...

   Started at the stillness broken by reply so aptly spoken...

   What this *grim, ungainly, ghastly, gaunt*, and ominous bird of yore...

Page 31: Using Alliteration

Student answers will vary. Possible answers include:

1. Lonely Linda lamented at the lake.

2. Silly Sally sliced snowflakes into silk.

3. Never nap when neighbors are noisy.

4. Ben believes baseball and basketball are boring.

5. My mom makes marvelous muffins.

Page 33: Identifying Assonance

1. Th<u>i</u>s <u>i</u>s the sh<u>i</u>p of pearl, wh<u>i</u>ch poets feign
2. I h<u>ea</u>r <u>e</u>ven now the infinite fi<u>e</u>rce chorus
3. On this gr<u>ee</u>n bank by the soft str<u>ea</u>m
4. Sl<u>ee</u>p sw<u>ee</u>tly in your humble graves

Page 33: Identifying Consonance

1. "Through the window<u>s</u>—through door<u>s</u>—bur<u>st</u> like a ruthle<u>ss</u> for<u>ce</u>."
2. "A <u>s</u>oul admitted to it<u>s</u>elf—<u>F</u>inite In<u>f</u>inity"
3. "<u>L</u>ies <u>s</u>tretching to my da<u>zz</u>led <u>s</u>ight A <u>l</u>uminou<u>s</u> be<u>l</u>t, a mi<u>s</u>ty <u>l</u>ight"
4. "And the poore<u>st</u> <u>t</u>wig of the elm <u>t</u>ree"

Page 34: Distinguishing Assonance from Consonance

1. Assonance: struck, luck
   Consonance: struck, streak
2. Assonance: hung, humble, button
   Consonance: heart, hung, humble
3. Assonance: silent, night, I
   Consonance: <u>s</u>ilent, re<u>st</u> (or) silen<u>t</u> nigh<u>t</u>, rest, <u>t</u>ook
4. Assonance: in, Nothing, Nothing, did, build
   Consonance: in, Nothing, and, Nothing

Page 36: Practicing Poetry

Student samples will vary, but should demonstrate understanding of the poetry forms.

Page 37: What's the Difference?

1. cinquain
2. haiku
3. limerick
4. Skeltonic verse

Page 39: Locating Onomatopoeia

The following words should be underlined:
1. rattle-rattle, rattle-rattle, Bing, boomlay, boomlay, boomlay, Boom, roaring
2. ooze, husha-husha-hush, slippery
3. roar, rushing
4. tinkle, tinkle, tinkle
5. blast, muttering, thunder, burst

Page 40: Hearing Onomatopoeia

A. 1. d; 2. a; 3. b; 4. c; 5. e

B. Student answers may vary, but might include: 1. shatter; 2. ding-dong; 3. clang; 4. shriek; 5. whisper, whistle, or whoosh

C. Student answers will vary.

Page 42: Locating Parallelism

Students should underline the following passages in Chief Joseph's speech: Our chiefs are killed. Looking Glass is dead. Toohoolhoolzote is dead. The old men are all dead. He who led on the young men is dead.

Students should underline everything except the first sentence in the Poe passage.

Page 42: Finding Mistakes in Parallelism

1. Karla went to the store and bought bread, peanut butter, and jelly.
2. Do check spelling. Do check grammar. Do check punctuation.
3. Kevin's hobbies include skiing, hiking, and reading.
4. Daisuke walked into the room. He put his briefcase down, poured himself some lemonade, and relaxed in his favorite chair.
5. The dog ran past the red bench, around the spiky bushes, and through the muddy river.

Page 43: Categorizing Types of Parallelism

1. b; 2. e; 3. d; 4. a; 5. c

Page 45: Reasons for Repetition

1. The refrain of the song repeats phrases to add both rhythm and emphasis to the sentiment of the refrain.

2. Thomas Paine repeats ideas to emphasize his points and persuade his readers.

3. Saki's quote uses repetition to create a pun.

4. The Maupassant quote uses repetition to create a sense of dread and exemplify stuttering.

Page 46: Using Repetition

Student answers will vary.

Page 48: Identifying Ending Rhyme Patterns

1. aa; 2. aabbcc; 3. abccb; 4. aabba; 5. abcb; 6. aabc

Page 49: Locating Internal Rhyme

Underline the following words: Mild, Smiled, Names, Games, Disgrace, Face, Pair, Everywhere, Gold, Told, Airs, Theirs, Old, Scold, Don't, Won't, Dine, Fine

Page 49: Writing Rhymes

Student answers will vary.

Page 51: Recognizing Regular Rhythms

1. meter
2. random rhythm
3. random rhythm
4. meter

Page 52: Writing Rhythm

Student responses will vary. Sample answers follow:

A. On Christmas morning, yesterday
My presents sat all neatly wrapped
Today the ribbons, bows, and tape
Lay scattered all across the map.

B. After hours,
alone in the classroom
the janitor sweeps and cleans
yet again.

Page 54: Distinguishing Between Poetry Line Types

1. run-on; 2. end-stopped; 3. end-stopped; 4. run-on; 5. end-stopped; 6. end-stopped; 7. run-on; 8. end-stopped; 9. run-on; 10. end-stopped

Page 55: Writing Run-on and End-stopped Lines

Student poems will vary, but should demonstrate understanding of run-on and end-stopped lines.

Page 57: Interpreting Stanzas

1. triplet
2. quatrain
3. septet
4. couplet
5. sestet
6. quintet

Page 58: Writing Poetry Stanzas

Student stanzas will vary, but should demonstrate understanding of couplets, triplets, and quatrains.

Page 60: Interpreting Allusions

1. The worker seemed heroic, quickly repairing the car and saving the day.

2. Cale is Mary's hero and romantic love-interest.

3. The protest was organized and well-attended and probably included posters and chants.

4. Kevin is creative, artistic, expert, and perhaps his art is abstract.

5. Yes, things get lost in Brian's room. We can tell because things disappear in a black hole.

6. Grandma bought the Christmas presents since she was referred to as Santa Claus.

Page 61: Appropriate Allusions

1. c; 2. d; 3. b; 4. e; 5. a

Page 61: Writing Allusions

Paragraphs will vary, but should demonstrate an understanding of allusions.

Page 63: Kinds of Characters

1. dynamic
2. flat
3. static
4. flat
5. round

Page 63: Characterization Methods

1. d; 2. a; 3. b; 4. c

Page 64: Creating Characters

Student responses will vary.

Page 66: Classifying Conflicts

1. a; 2. e; 3. c; 4. b; 5. d; 6. e; 7. a; 8. d

Page 67: Creating Conflicts

Student responses will vary, but should demonstrate an understanding of conflict types.

Page 69: Interpreting Dialect

A.

1. If you haven't read *The Adventures of Tom Sawyer*, you don't know me; but that doesn't matter.

2. Hi, brother, where's my nephew? Is he the one who arranged for this band?

3. Time marched on from Christmas to Easter to the month of May when plants began to bloom.

4. The whole thing will be settled now because Lacy Bassett is coming down to look things over.

B.

1. You are beautiful, my dear. I love you now and will continue to do so until all the seas go dry.

2. "Well," Smiley said calmly, "I figure he's good enough to outjump any frog in Calaveras County."

Page 70: Identifying Dialect

1. c; 2. a; 3. d; 4. b; 5. e

Page 70: Unscrambling Dialect

1. "On Top of Old Smokey"

2. "Twinkle, Twinkle, Little Star"

Page 72: Identifying the Purpose of Dialogue

1. b,c; 2. e; 3. a; 4. d

Page 73: Writing Dialogue

Student responses will vary.

Page 75: Why Flack Back?

Student responses will vary.

Page 75: Find the Flahback

Students should underline "On the evening... by her talk."

Page 76: Writing a Flashback

Student stories will vary.

Page 78: Foreshadowing in Fairy Tales

Answers must be in complete sentences.

Page 79: Rewriting "The Ugly Duckling"

Student stories will vary.

Page 81: Categorizing Genres

Nonfiction prose: essay, biography, letter, persuasive speech, report

Fiction prose: historical fiction, science fiction, horror, fantasy, mystery

Poetry: epic, lyric, nature poem, free verse, sonnet

Drama: screenplay, comedy, melodrama, farce, tragedy

Page 81: Identifying Genres

1. farce; 2. horror; 3. persuasive speech;
4. fantasy

Page 81: Using Genres Effectively

1. essay; 2. historical fiction; 3. science fiction

Page 82: Matching Genres

1. e; 2. b; 3. f; 4. c; 5. a; 6. d; 7. g

Page 84: Understanding Irony

1. The man is not hunting animals at all, but humans. Additionally, it is he who is dangerous because he is insane.

2. All the work the woman did to buy an expensive necklace was not necessary since she was replacing an imitation.

3. Student responses will vary, but should convey that irony is the difference between what happens and what you expect to happen.

4. Student responses will vary.

Page 84: Predicting Irony

1. The ugly duckling is not a duck at all, but rather a swan.

2. The man is arrested for loitering.

Page 85: Identifying Irony

1. verbal irony

2. situational irony

3. dramatic irony

4. The policeman survived incredible odds (perhaps for years) only to be killed by a freak accident.

Page 85: Using Irony

Student responses will vary.

Page 87: Locating Local Color

1. dialect; 2. clothing, mannerisms, customs;
3. scenery, attitudes

Page 88: Creating Local Color

Student responses will vary.

Page 90: Recognizing Mood and Tone

1. humorous; 2. serious; 3. humorous;
4. serious

Page 91: Matching Tones and Moods

1. remorseful; 2. fearful; 3. lighthearted;
4. gloomy; 5. hopeless

Page 93: Concluding a Moral

It is best to prepare for the days of necessity. Little friends may prove great friends.

Page 94: Writing Morals

Student responses will vary.

Page 94: Recognizing Theme

1. Beauty is only skin deep. Love conquers all.

2. Be yourself, even if you are unusual.

3. Friends work together.

4. It pays to be truthful.

5. Ignore stereotypes. Differences don't matter.

Page 96: Identifying Points of View

1. second; 2. third; 3. third; 4. second; 5. first; 6. first

Page 97: Using Narration

Student responses will vary.

Page 97: Using Using Point of View

Student responses will vary.

Page 99: Identifying Parts of a Plot

Answers appear in this order: (3) climax, (1) exposition, (2) rising action, (5) resolution, (4) falling action

Page 100: Developing a Plot

Student responses will vary.

Page 102: Locating Poetic License Usage

Student responses will vary.

Page 103: License to Create

Student responses will vary.

Page 105: Understanding Puns

1. The pun about light is funny because *light* can mean both the absence of darkness and the opposite of heavy. When Milo ordered a square meal, "the waiters reappeared carrying plates heaped with steaming squares of all shapes and sizes."

2. Puns are funny because the reader is expecting one thing and gets something slightly different, but curiously similar.

3. Puns may have first appeared when innocent mistakes in pronunciation were made.

Page 105: Punny Jokes

A. 1. similar sounding words; 2. different meanings; 3. similar sounding words

B. 1. spoiled milk; 2. chocolate milk; 3. a milk shake; 4. buttermilk

Page 106: Writing Puns

A. 1. e; 2. j; 3. f; 4. i; 5. h; 6. b; 7. c; 8. d; 9. g; 10. a

B. Answers will vary.

Page 108: Interpreting Rhetorical Questions

1. The British have made no steps toward accepting the colonists as equals in the past ten years.

2. We have reasoned with the British long enough. They do not listen to reason.

3. We have attempted to compromise with the British. They do not accept our terms.

4. We need to fight now, whether we feel ready or not, because if we wait, we will only be further repressed by the British.

5. We cannot stay out of war out of fear because life is not worth living in the absence of freedom.

Page 109: Using Rhetorical Questions

Student answers will vary, but possible answers follow:

1. Have you ever traveled to Paris through the pages of a book?

2. What kinds of jobs do high school dropouts get?

3. How many nationalities do you meet on one block of a Los Angeles street?

4. Have you ever danced to a Spanish song?

5. Do you think anyone would have thought up the button if he wasn't tired of doing up all those metal hooks?

6. Isn't homework easier when you complete it with a friend?

7. Have you ever acted too soon only to learn something didn't really need to be done?

8. How many wrist watches have you replaced in the last year?

Page 111: Categorizing Satires, Parodies, and Farces

1. farce; 2. parody; 3. parody; 4. satire; 5. satire

Page 112: Writing Satires, Parodies, and Farces

Student responses will vary.

Page 114: Locating a Story Within a Story

"John Brown, aged thirty-one, good, gentle, bashful, timid, lived in a quiet village in Missouri."

Page 115: Interpreting a Story Within a Story

1. Sailors were the main characters in the framework story.

2. The main conflict in the framework story is how to end a story that one of the sailors tells.

3. John Brown and Mary Taylor are likely to be the main characters in the inner story.

4. The inner story probably takes over because it is humorous and suspenseful. Twain probably set it in a framework story only to give him a plot technique that would allow the story to not have an end.

5. Student responses will vary.

Page 117: Understanding Stream of Consciousness

1. Children experience things in disconnected ways and often talk about them as such.

2. Student answers will vary. Possible answers might include a story with a rushed mood, a first-person account of an experience with madness, or a story that requires reader interpretation rather than author interpretation.

Page 117: Explaining Stream of Consciousness

1. The repetition of "Do I dare?" makes it clear the author is thinking aloud. The jump from the fact that the author is balding to the idea of what people will say about that is a flow that might occur in the natural thinking process.

2. The author states things quickly and simply, as they occur to him.

Page 118: Identifying Stream of Consciousness

1 and 4

Page 120: Predicting Surprise Endings

1. Mr. Easton was the criminal, not the sheriff.

2. The man learns that he himself has died.

3. The letter is from Sam, who says he found the third level and is living in 1894.

Page 121: Writing the Rest

Answers will vary.

Page 123: Questioning Suspense

1. a. Why was Moxon speaking with such earnestness?; b. Why did Moxon let no one into the machine-shop?; c. What was the sound?

2. a. Will a tragedy follow? What tragedy?; b. Will the narrator be able to help his friend? How will he help his friend?

Page 123: Identifying Suspense Tools

1. dark setting

2. mysterious characters

3. difficult decision

4. mysterious circumstances

5. unresolved issue

Page 124: Locating Suspense

Students may underline different passages, but the ones they choose should demonstrate an understanding of suspense tools.

Pages 125–126: Review: Literary Terms and Techniques

1. b
2. a
3. c
4. b
5. d
6. c
7. d
8. b
9. a
10. d
11. c
12. d
13. d
14. d
15. a
16. b
17. d
18. a, b, c
19. a
20. a